"If I Grow a Beard, Do I Have to Dye That, Too?" And Other Questions I Want to Ask God About Menopause

Copyright 2013, Heather Nestleroad

Print ISBN # 978-0-9860059-7-8

First edition - January 2014

"If I Grow a Beard, Do I Have to Dye That, Too?" And Other Questions I Want to Ask God About Menopause

Copyright 2013, Heather Nestleroad

All rights reserved. This book may not be reproduced in any form, in whole or in part, without written permission from the author.

ISBN # 978-0-9860059-5-4 EPUB edition

ISBN # 978-0-9860059-6-1 Kindle edition

ISBN # 978-0-9860059-7-8 Paperback

Published in the USA by PublishSavvy
Editing by Shannon Janeczek

Layout, formatting and book design by PublishSavvy
Cover design by Karen Nowosatko
Line drawings by Elizabeth Harner

All Bible quotes are from the Life Application Study Bible, New International Version, 1991.

Dedication

For my perfect little angels*, "Daphne," "Megan," and "Scotty":
I love you to the moon and back and everywhere in between.

For my sweetheart, "Vaughn": You complete me.

And, of course, to mom. I miss you.

All names have been changed to protect the not-so-innocent, innocents.

Table of Contents

Introduction

Section 1

Letter to Mom: I'm 40	5
Question: If I Grow a Beard, Do I Have to Dye That, Too?	6
The Big 4-0	9
Finding Focus	13
You Know You Are Old When	15
Kittens & God	18
How the Social Network Makes Us Less Social	21
God Uses All of Us	24
How I Became an Actual Writer	27
Getting Out of My Zone	30
Keeping Up Appearances	33
Coffee Shop or Library	36
Tim McGraw Day	49
Why Is Underwear So Expensive If No One Ever Sees It?	41
A Lot Can Happen While in the Bathroom	44
The Urologist's Office	47
Unwanted Visitors	50

Section 2

Letter to Mom: An Update	53
Question: What Are You Doing With Your One and Only Life?	56
What Are You Waiting For? GO!	58

My Son's Multiple Careers	61
You Might Have a Little Teeny Tiny Bit of Road Rage If…	63
The Best You Can Be	66
WebMD, Go Away!	68
Who's Driving the Boat?	70
Cheeseburgers	72
Was That a Burp or Is a Large Truck Stopping Outside?	75
Christmas Reflections	77
The End of the World As We Know It	80
Setting the Standard for What Not to Wear	83
Best Friend	85
Miss Congeniality	88
In the Middle of Middle-Aged	91

Section 3

Letter to Mom: Menopause	94
Question: Can You Schedule a Hysterectomy?	96
I'm Getting Too Old for This	98
Expressions	102
Siri	105
Green Eggs & Ham	108
Are You There, Menopause? It's me, Heather.	111
Fixed	113
Go Forth and Multiply	115
If the Dryer Only Dries On Hot, Is It Really the Ice Cream's Fault?	117

Real-Life Designer Bathing Suits	119
Poo Spray	121
Shopping & the Black Van	123
Life with Estrogen	126
Fire Engine Red	128
Drama & the Sermon on the Bed	131

Section 4

Letter to Mom: Short Hair	135
Question: Is It OK Not to Shave Your Legs in the Winter?	136
Marketing Meeting	138
Sweet or Mean?	140
Shape Up or Ship Out	142
Keeping it Real	144
Changing the View	148
The Birds & the Bees	151
Boundaries	153
Sweating Like a Turkey the Week Before Thanksgiving	156
Self-Control	159
Dust Bunnies - Ya Gotta Love 'Em	162
How Much Protection Do We Really Need?	164
Pharmacist's Wife	166

Section 5

Letter to Mom: Birthday	171
Question: If They Don't Get Older in the Scrapbook, Does That Mean They Will Never Leave?	173
Being the Bad Guy, or Why I Might Start Drinking	176

The Mind of Megan	180
Fan Girl	183
What's the Eighteenth Year?	186
The 500-Month Birthday	190
Stretch Marks Need A New Publicist	192
Daphne, Wallflowers and Wanting to Die	194
It's Elementary, My Dear	196
Counting Chickens	198
Thankful	200
Laser Tag	202
Toothbrushes	205
Time Keeps on Slipping, Slipping	208
History Channel	210
What Kind of Christian?	212
Wardrobe Malfunction	214
Joyful	216
Lost & Found, or, a Note from the Author	218
Acknowledgements	222

About the Author

Introduction

Consider this fair warning. The book you are holding in your hand was written under the influence. During the writing of this book, God was with me. Coffee drinks that have more sugar than actual coffee were present, and a significant amount of gum was chewed.

This book is a journey, a collection of stories about my family, and my walk with God. The only time that I will get scientific in this book is when I contemplate if there really is a difference between liquid measuring cups and dry measuring cups. (I still do not know the answer, by the way.)

I will answer a few questions right away. I *do* think I'm a little bit funny. In the sense that God took an only child, from a divorced, dysfunctional family and chose to give her the full family experience as an adult. I grew up without an ally. There were no kids against the parents when I grew up; it was me against the world, alone… at least as I saw it. The fact is, if I look back, I can see that not once was I alone.

My journey as a parent of teenage girls, when I didn't like teenage girls (and I was one of them once!) is funny. My journey as a parent of a boy, when I didn't know anything about boys, is funny. I in no way claim to be a comedian, but sometimes I crack myself up. My journey is funny to me. My kids crack me up. Life cracks me up. Mostly because I have nothing figured out…still.

The way I see it, you can find the funny, or you can spend your life in devastation. I saw that side. I lived that side. But I don't live there anymore.

How did I get to that point? I am the female equivalent of Jonah. If I'm told to go to Nineveh, I'm going through the whale — I'm taking the longest, most painful route to get there, because to go straight to the destination would be too easy. I am a work in progress. I relish the fact that God isn't finished with me yet. But I still look forward to the journey, no matter the route, because I know that at the end of these travels is going to be Paradise. Of this, I am certain.

So if you cannot type or read the name of my Father God, this isn't the book for you. If you cannot laugh at yourself, much less anyone else, this isn't the book for you.

I should also warn you that I did write most of this braless, and in sweats. That's the secret of my success. Sweats, gum and coffee.

Enjoy!

— *Heather*

Section 1

Dear Mom,

As you know, I turned forty this last year; a fact that I'm sure you would have enjoyed. Maybe not as much as I would have enjoyed you turning sixty, but that is neither here nor there.

As I approach the next decade, I have many questions that I would have liked to have asked you. I have decided to write letters to you so I can get my questions out there, and maybe someone who reads them will bless me with the answers.

OK, I distinctly remember grandma having some facial hair. Did she not take hormones, or is this something I am going to have to look forward to? I'm sure you understand my concern. Although I am not quite as hairy as you were. I don't have arm hair and you did have that odd long hair on your arm that I once tried to pull off not realizing that it was attached.

I do have some concern, however, about my eyebrows. While my eyebrows do not quite grow like they once did, I am finding odd strays that I have to pluck on the bridge of my nose sometimes, and lower, towards my eyelid. I have nightmares about waking up with a unibrow like that woman on the "Dodgeball" movie and it is not attractive.

When did this odd hair thing start? Is this a family trait that I cannot avoid, or might I bypass it and take off of dad's side of the family, as they seem to be less hairy?

Just curious, and (still) wishing you were here.

Love,

Heather

Question:
If I Grow a Beard, Do I Have to Dye That, Too?

I have crossed over to the forties. In doing that, I have also begun the countdown to menopause. Crazy, I know.

Menopause is a funny word. What are they saying? Pause-o-men! Pause to become men? Men-o-pause! I'm not sure if I'm going to turn into a man or if I should just halt my man's advances till it passes, but how can it pass if it's paused? The entire thing is confusing.

I was thinking I would be saving money when I finally get there, because I won't have to purchase any more feminine hygiene products. Then I realized I would have to buy products to keep me from growing a beard, so when I go out with my husband, people can tell us apart. We have been married for 18 years at this point, and it's true that you start looking like each other after a while. I got rounder, so did he. My hair got darker to match his; it also got shorter, so it doesn't take long to fix. We are already close to the same height. He's about three inches taller, unless I wear heels.

When my daughters were younger, I bought them a book about what was happening to their bodies during puberty. Are there books like this for menopause, with cute cartoons? If so, do they read more like a horror story, or a fairy tale that has no cramping and no periods?

(I will admit that I am a read-for-entertainment girl. Textbooks, or books that teach you how to knit, or work a computer program, are not my thing. I am a learn-by-doing kind of girl. I taught myself how to knit once because I sat and watched someone knit).

I have a lot of questions. Like, will I finally warm up? I am usually cold. I love summer, because I get to thaw out. If I start having hot flashes, it could be a relief in the wintertime.

In the summer, I might not make it, though; I pass out if I overheat. Maybe I will lose weight from sweating so much and not eating (because I'm unconscious half the time).

My mother is gone, so I don't have her experience to draw from. In fact, I don't remember her going through it. She was fifty-two when she went home to be with Jesus. I'm not sure if she was done with menopause or if she was in the midst of it.

I don't remember her opening windows in the middle of the winter because she was hot. She was always a size four, so she didn't gain weight. She was beautiful, always. She didn't have a mustache or beard, although my grandmother on that side did have a bit of a mustache. I would not like to inherit that bit. I already have their thighs, among other things. The mustache I can do without.

Although… if I do grow facial hair, do I have to dye that too? I already color the hair on top of my head because I am far too young to have any silver sparklers happening. I already have to go to the store and buy the foamy hair color every six weeks or so. How often would I have to dye a beard?

And it's one more color to keep track of. I never remember what color I bought before. I just pick whatever looks pretty that day. One month I may be a chocolate brown, and the next I may be a mahogany chocolate brown. I may have made that one up. But I do like to pick colors with the word chocolate in them, because, who doesn't like chocolate? I picked the color of my deck because it was called chocolate. If peanut butter hair color were an option, I would have to learn to give myself highlights.

If you are a woman with a mustache and you highlight your hair, do you put highlights in your mustache too, so it matches? If you shave it, do you have to worry about a five o'clock shadow? How does this all work? How fast is this imminent hair going to grow? How fast do the "stop the facial hair" drugs work? Is it an immediate satisfaction kind of thing, or does it take a couple weeks to really kick in? If anyone has any answers to these questions, I'd really appreciate it.

The Big 4-0

I'm 40. When did that happen? I mean, I know the date of my birthday. I know it happened, I just cannot figure out when I got to be so old.

When I was a kid, I remember having to go to bed at 9 p.m. I remember having to be home before dark. I remember wishing time would pass faster so I could have my driver's license. Today, my daughter was driving ME around. Granted, I was telling her to stay in her lines, like she was coloring, and nagging her to remember the brake, but still, she was driving me, and not the other way around.

I used to dream of the day when I would leave home. I would go to Chicago, live in the big city, and never come home again. I would be very chic and I would have lots of friends and ride in taxis. When I was a teenager, I don't think I ever aged in my imagination past twenty. I didn't even dream of turning 21, because I was never interested in drinking.

Up until the second semester of my senior year, I didn't fantasize of having a husband and children either, but that changed when I met my future husband. Then I did dream of being married. (The children part came shortly after we got married, when he looked at me crosswise and I got pregnant.)

I don't think anyone dreams of what life will be like at forty. Teenagers don't think, "When I'm forty, I'm going to ... sail around the world." Or "When I'm forty, I'm going to learn how to play backgammon." It's just not done.

This is forty.

My hair is short. My hair has been short for a while now, but in my family when we women get old, we cut our hair. There is a side of my hair that grows faster and thicker than the other, and the back tends to flip up.

I have now been every size between a size 3 to a 16. There are parts of my body that have fallen and need extra support to stay up. Spandex is my friend.

I wonder if my freckles are still considered freckles, or if they will become age spots.

My eyebrows no longer grow like they used to; there are only random strays here and there that I pluck out.

I use Clinique, but wonder if I shouldn't be using Oil of Olay (AKA, Oil of Old Lady) instead.

I say the phrase "Well, how 'bout that!" all the time now. I have surpassed sounding like my mother and have gone straight to sounding like my grandmother. (I think that makes me an overachiever, doesn't it?)

My daughter, had she had a less dramatic mother, should have her license by now. She doesn't, because I have been too afraid to let her drive me around. I'm getting a little better about it. Maybe when she is seventeen, I will even let her drive at night, or when it rains... or, maybe not. I may need a little longer. *She* may need a little longer. My middle child is right behind her; she will have driver's ed next summer. And she was just learning how to ride a bike last week. OK, no, it was a minute ago.

My baby? My baby is in double digits. DOUBLE DIGITS! He's my baby. I know I was rocking him to sleep just yesterday. Today I turn around and I am only a head taller than he is. Granted, I'm not especially tall, but still.

In the blink of an eye, it's not me learning to drive, and it isn't me dreaming of leaving home and going off to college, or even just driving to the mall alone.

My dreams are more along the lines of going up the stairs without my knees creaking. Wondering how long I can go between coloring my hair. If I don't color my hair, how long until my entire head is grey? Will I be 45? 50? 60? Will I be doing commercials for urinary incontinence? If I work at the school long enough, will it be "grandma hugs" I give the children, or will I still be able to give mommy hugs when I get older?

I have become one of the biggest clichés in motherhood. When I take the kids out for recess at school, I yell at them to stay off the grass and stay on the sidewalk till we get onto the playground. I ask my children if they were born in barns; I have said "Close the door! I don't want to [heat/air condition] the outdoors." This last weekend I went on a date with my husband and I reached over with a napkin to wipe his face. (This did not earn me any favors.)

Where did the time go? It seems to pass so quickly. Days run over each other. When I was younger, the time seemed to pass so slowly. I thought I would never get grown. Now I'm grown and all I want is for time to slow down. Weeks are suddenly months that are gone, and years are gone in a blink. I look in the mirror and I see wrinkles that weren't there before. I look at my children and I am looking up instead of down to look into their eyes. Even our cats seem to be aging rapidly.

When we start out, we think we have so much time, to do so many things. The fact is, we don't know how much time we have. The older we get, the less we have. We have to decide how we are going to spend what we have. I think I will spend mine enjoying the teenagers who tell me I'm old.

I will keep searching for the perfect hair color, and refuse to grow my hair out. I don't want to wear buns, and I will continue to avoid skirts, skorts, and dresses because they go well with aprons. I will enjoy my jam sessions when I'm home alone. Maybe I will need Depends someday, but doesn't that just mean I get to dance longer without stopping because I don't have to "go gotta go, gotta go, right now"?

The sun shines brighter when you look at every day as a gift. Maybe forty won't be so bad. After all, I have a new haircut, and I

can blow big bubbles, even with Trident gum. The up side is, I'm old enough that I don't have to apologize for enjoying it.

Finding Focus

My daughter is having trouble driving. Or maybe it's more a matter that my husband and I are having a problem with her driving. She is terrifying us. I recently had a discussion with a driver's ed instructor and he told me that if she is choking the wheel, she is probably looking directly in front of her and not looking down the road, which is why she overcorrects.

This got me to thinking about how often we tend to just look at what is in front of us, and not what is down the road. Where the road will take us is a mystery, unless we are looking farther down the road.

I remember being a teenager many years ago. I was more concerned with what I was doing on the weekend than with what I was going to do with my life. I think that is where many find themselves even as they grow older. What are we going to do this weekend? What are we going to do for dinner? What are we going to do tomorrow? Often, it doesn't occur to us to think about what we are going to do five years from now. Goals are not made. Planning doesn't occur. In an immediate-satisfaction society, we are more concerned with the here and now, instead of next week or next year. We don't concern ourselves with how decisions today will affect us in the future.

There are so many things that I would have done differently then, now that I am older. With my own teenagers, I try to express to them how fast high school goes by, then it is gone. Never will you go back to always being with your parents and depending on them for your needs. While you are in college, you will get glimpses of what the future will hold and things that prepare you for what is to come.

When Jesus was with the disciples, he taught them in parables or stories to help them to understand more easily what was to come and how things were to be. I try to tell my kids stories from when I was younger. They do not seem to think it relates to them, and I haven't a clue if anything is sinking in. I wonder if Jesus ever felt like his disciples were just not getting it, or being Jesus, he knew already what was going to happen (that they were going to get it in the end).

I am certain that when dealing with me, sometimes God just shakes his head and thinks "She just cannot do what I tell her the first time." Although He has the benefit of knowing what I am going to do before I do it, and he knows that eventually I will get there. If only I could know that the girls were going to get it at some point, and that when the time comes, they will have it all together. I hope they will be able to function in society without me being there every step of the way.

Of course, I will always be there for my children when they need me, but they are going to have to make decisions for themselves. They are going to be responsible. The time for looking down the road, and not just at the road directly in front of us, is now. Whether I like it or not, college, jobs, marriage and children are in their futures, and I have to accept that they are not my babies anymore. The girls are becoming young women; hopefully, the young women that God wants them to be. I can only hope that they will get to the place that God has planned for them, without going through the proverbial whale like I always do.

So where is your focus? Are you focusing on the here and now, or are you looking down the road? Are you planning for the future and looking to God to be your guide? It can be scary to think that far into the future. In every aspect of my life—be it with my husband, my children, or my career—I have been far happier looking to the future, planning and seeking wisdom than I ever was living for the here and now. Sometimes, in this 4G world, it helps to take the time to smell the roses, instead of just looking at the screen.

You Know You Are Old When…

I am not sure what my natural hair color is now. I have been coloring my hair for some time. It began when my second child was born. My mother looked at me and asked me what I was doing to my hair. At that time, I hadn't colored my hair; my hair had naturally gotten darker with childbirth. I'm not sure which was more shocking to me: the fact that I had been a blonde that went to light brown as an adult to a dark brown with childbirth, or the fact that my feet grew a half size for each child I had, and I could no longer smell properly after giving birth to them.

I started with highlights to make my mother happy. She wanted her blonde child back. This lasted a few years, but then the highlights turned my entire head blonde and the upkeep became more than I had time to handle. Then I started going darker and I would just let the hairdresser choose a color. Now I have more grey hair than I have cash to pay for the upkeep of that, too. So I use an at-home foamy kit and color it myself.

My hair color is now a medium chocolate brown. Sometimes I stray in the summer and try a different color, but for the most part I have decided this is the color. Mostly because it takes too much thought to keep changing it and keeping track of what color I did the time before.

I now say things like "When I was a kid, we went outside to play. We didn't have all of these electronic gadgets to play with. This is why everyone is so overweight; no one goes outside anymore."

And "You better be careful or your face will freeze that way." Are these proclamations something that one just inherits with age? Do you get a new one with each new grey hair? If I keep coloring my hair, can I erase them and sound cool again?

Sometimes I think I have an ulcer from the stress of dealing with the constant teenage girl drama. I am certain I am doing something wrong. There is no way that I am not messing this up. God gave me these beautiful creatures and there is no way it could be them that is the problem; it has to be me. I am a failure as a parent and now I have grey hair to highlight my wrongdoing in the parenting department.

I do not like to wear heels. If you come to an event and I am wearing heels, just know I did so under protest. Clarks are my new favorite shoes because they are comfortable. They make my feet so happy. I just turned forty and I am wearing Clarks. It's not like I'm wearing Soft Spots yet, so it's OK, right? Clark has some stylish shoes. I started wearing Aerosoles in college, then I had a brief stint with stylish but uncomfortable shoes. Now I am back to comfort. Where my peers are in love with flip-flops, I look at them and see pain. There's no arch support in those things.

The world is a different place now. There are abbreviations for things I don't know about. Telephones fit in pockets and tell you the weather and can give you movie times. Books are electronic, and you can carry your entire music collection in your pocket. While a lot of the things that are designed to make life easier are great, sometimes I do miss things from my youth. I introduced my children to the eighties, just so I would have someone to enjoy my youth with. I wish I still had a typewriter so I could show them the "computer" of my day.

So how do you know you are getting old? I guess it is when you realize your children are getting older, and know more about some things than you do. Also, I think it is when your kids start telling you that you are old, and the mirror agrees. There are days when I swear it isn't my reflection but my mother's in the mirror. The store I once loved to buy clothes in, I look in and think, "Wow, I could never wear half the things in here anymore." Pants should cover parts that no one needs to see. Low-rise jeans are for people who have never given birth.

Yeah I'm getting older. But I think I'm OK with that. I do remember being younger. It wasn't always all it was cracked up to be. Also, I think that getting older makes it so that I can enjoy things more. As you get older, you take things for granted less.

Young people know the difference between Microsoft Word and Microsoft Word Processor and don't get excited when they figure out the difference, for example. Not that I know anyone like that.

Kittens & God

One Saturday morning, as I was walking by my front door, I happened to notice that there was a kitten sitting on my porch. This is interesting, as the two cats I already own are geriatric, so they're unable to reproduce. The kitten, who has been named Kitty Purry (mostly because the girls and I had gone to see the Katy Perry movie earlier in the week), is still residing on my porch.

I decided, even with my hair a fright, and my Thing 1 and Thing 2 pajamas on, I should go out there to meet this new member of my family. But of course, as soon as I opened the door and stepped out, the kitten startled away. I then decided it would be a good idea to call for the kitten, and walk around the yard to try and find it. It was early, so it didn't occur to me that any of my neighbors would see me. I was incorrect.

As I am walking around, calling for this kitten that I can't see because it had hidden itself quite deeply within a large bush in my front yard, a neighbor happened by to witness this event. She was pushing her one year old in a stroller walking past my house. She gave me a look, and I looked down at myself and said, "Hello! Uh yeah, this is weekend wear, right?"

She smiled, "Yeah, sure."

I followed with, "I'm looking for a kitten, you see. It just showed up. Do you know anyone who is missing one? It looks like the cat we had, that died seven years ago."

She didn't know anyone who was missing a kitten and probably silently hoped her son wouldn't make eye contact, so they could get home as quickly as they could.

I can only imagine what she was thinking. Perhaps something like, "Is this what happens to you when you get older? Do teenagers do that to you? Does she really believe that there is a cat? I don't see a cat. I wonder if she thinks she IS the cat, since she is wearing Thing 1 and Thing 2 pajamas. I think I've seen her dancing while she mows the yard. Maybe if I pretend I don't see her next time, she won't engage."

Or maybe she thought the scene before her was perfectly natural. She does dress up as a Disney Princess on Halloween. We call her Cinderella at our house. She is quite lovely and very kind. She would have to be, to converse with the crazy lady in pajamas calling for a kitten she can't see.

I go outside and talk to the kitten. I bought some kitten food for it. I sang "Jesus Loves Me." I implore the kitten to trust me, to come to me, and let me be her mama. I promise the kitten that I will not hurt her, and that I only want to be her friend and take care of her. I tell her about the kids. Then the kids go out and talk to her. I tell her about the two cats we already own, even though the cats run from her. Yet the kitten still won't come to me.

Then... the light bulb moment happens.

You, I'm sure, saw this coming long before I did. It sort of snuck up on me. I was just holding my hand out to the kitten and singing "The Lord Is My Shepherd," and it occurred to me. Is this how my Father feels? He wants us to come to Him to trust Him to let Him take care of us, and what do we do? We scurry away. Why? Does He understand why we do it?

For the life of me, I cannot understand what is wrong with this cat. I feed her, I make sure she has water, I do everything I can, and the thing will just not come to me. I don't make any sudden movements. I don't try to grab her, and have her not trust me. Why does she not get it? Why do I not get it? Why do we not get it, together?

I'm not sure of the answer. I only know that my Father wants me to come to him. He wants me to trust Him. He wants me to let Him take care of me. And you know what? I am tired of running away.

Proverbs 3:5: "Trust the LORD with all your heart; and lean not on your own understanding." I don't need to understand; I just need to trust.

How the Social Network Makes Us Less Social

When I was growing up, we didn't have cell phones. We learned to type on a typewriter. If we wanted to talk to someone, we had to call them on the phone that was mounted to the wall, or we had to go to their house and knock on the door.

Today my kids do not know a world without the World Wide Web, everyone has a cell phone, and they have never seen a typewriter. This is sad, because they are also slow typers because of it.

It used to be that if you wanted a short cut in writing, you took shorthand. You didn't have the texting jargon that they have today. While at one time I could read and take shorthand at sixty words a minute, I no longer remember a bit of it. I wish I could, because I believe the kids would be just as impressed with that as they once were with my two phrases of French (all I remember from two years of French class). You know, before one of them became a third-year Spanish student, I was a rock star with those two phrases. Now they just laugh at me because I don't know Spanish.

Today we have cell phones with texting and the Social Network. I have heard that boys don't even call and ask girls out anymore. They text them to ask them on dates, or they talk to them on Facebook. With Facebook, MySpace, Twitter (and all the other networks that I don't even know the names of), we have created an entire generation of social illiterates. People have no idea how to have conversations. Think about it.

Kids rarely even knock on doors to play anymore. Phone calls have to be made and play dates arranged. Only now that my son is ten do I see the boys in the neighborhood coming to the door and asking to play. When I was a kid, we more often than not invited ourselves over. In fact, I would have to say that that probably saved my life more than once. I spent the night at friend's houses regularly; I stayed for dinner, regularly. Now we have gotten so busy we have to check a calendar to see if we can have a friend over for the night. It's sad.

I am a little concerned that my daughters may never date. It's because I won't let them go on a date with a boy unless he calls or comes over, and then asks them to go on the date. If the boy isn't man enough to call and ask for the date in real life, he isn't worthy of my daughter. If he is too scared of my daughter, he is going to be terrified of me, because he will also be forced to meet me and my husband before they go.

Has this technology helped with interpersonal relationships? Sure, we are connected, but do IKR and TTYL and LOL and BTDT really count as a full conversation? Isn't it better to LOL in person? Do we not lose the joy of the sound of laughter if the people we are talking to are at the other end of a computer? If you have the flu and the phones are static-filled and the only form of communication is through a computer... fine. I get it.

I have Facebook. I don't tweet, but I have Twitter. I have my first smart phone but I don't use half of what it is capable of. I do like having the weather at my fingertips. I also like the game Seven Little Words.

If there comes a day that I stop calling people on the phone, or meeting with friends for lunch, or to "play" bunko (I say "play" in quotes, because for the last few months we have spent all of our time together just snacking and talking), then I would like to ask someone to take all of these devices away from me. There is no substitution for talking to someone in person. There is no substitution for the joy one gets from the hug of a friend.

If you define joy with any electronic device, then I am sorry for what our society has created. We have things like Facetime and Facebook to stay in contact with people who are far away, not so we don't have to have any contact with the human race if we don't want to.

God created us to be social beings, to love one another and to help each other. To really connect and laugh and giving someone a hug when they need it cannot be done appropriately through a text message. Make plans to meet for dinner. Make plans to go have a cup of coffee or a soda and catch up. Create a book club, a bunko group, a dinner club, or do something that gets you off of the computer and into the company of the ones you like to spend time with. Do something that fills a conversation with love and grace.

Jesus didn't text people and arrange a meeting. He went out and met the people where they were. He went out and loved them and talked with them and taught them what it means to love and to have a conversation. So let's replicate his example and spread the Word!

God Uses All of Us

Some time ago there was a picture of sorts going around on Facebook. This is what it said:

<u>Do You Seriously Think God Can't Use You?</u>
Noah was a drunk
Abraham was too old
Isaac was a daydreamer
Jacob was a liar
Leah was ugly
Joseph was abused
Moses had a stuttering problem
Gideon was afraid
Samson had long hair and was a womanizer
Rahab was a prostitute
Jeremiah and Timothy were too young
David had an affair and was a murderer
Elijah was suicidal
Isaiah preached naked
Jonah ran from God

Naomi was a widow

Job went bankrupt

Peter denied Christ

The disciples fell asleep while praying

Martha worried about everything

The Samaritan woman was divorced

Zaccheus was too small

Paul was too religious

Timothy had an ulcer

Lazarus was dead

This was followed by 1Corinthians 1:26-29, which says, "Think of what you were when you were called. Not many of you were wise by human standards; not many were influential; not many were of noble birth. But God chose the foolish things of the world to shame the wise; God chose the weak things of the world to shame the strong. God chose the lowly things of this world and the despised things - and the things that are not - to nullify the things that are, so that no one may boast before him."

In church recently, we were discussing the choices of God and that is what crossed my mind. I have struggled. I am a daydreamer and I have trouble focusing. I'm great at procrastinating. I have lied, I was verbally abused as a child by my stepfather, I am afraid of public speaking, I am afraid of failure, and success, I am afraid of heights, I have even come up with several ways I would kill myself (obviously I figured out that was a bad idea). I have fallen asleep praying, hoping God knows what I wish to express to him, even if I fall asleep in the middle of it. I worry that I am not doing everything that I can do to take care of my family and my job and my house, or not doing what God wants me to do, or if I am, I'm not doing it well. I am afraid of being a disappointment.

When the pastor talked about God's choices to use those people despite their flaws, I thought of myself. Who am I? I'm no one special. I don't have a big-time degree, I'm not successful in business by society's standards, I'm not even so versed in the Bible that I know all the locations of the passages I know.

I don't know how I could be the person to teach anyone anything. There are so many people in the world that are far better prepared and equipped than I am for whatever life or God may throw their way. I would describe myself as a big chicken, who worries that all of her chicks may be damaged because she sat on them too long to protect them from the world.

But it occurs to me that maybe all of that is OK. Maybe God is choosing me for something that is beyond my understanding. I don't have to understand his choice to use me. I just have to be willing to be used. Maybe I have a story that could help someone to find God in their life as well. Maybe God could give me words to say and others could come to know him through me. That is the commission, right? I may be broken, but I think if I really investtigated, I would be hard-pressed to find someone who had it ALL together and was perfect.

Do I not tell my children that while I love them, there has only ever been one perfect person on this earth and they are not them? Jesus was the only one who was perfect and he still is to this day. I guess it's not about being perfect. I don't have to be. Maybe the fact that I'm not is part of God's plan.

Do you think that God can't use you? I believe He can, and He will, if you will let him. If you are willing to let go of what or who you think God's choice should be, and come to the understanding that God's choices are not our own, you will see clearly that He always makes the right choice. Sometimes His choice is you.

How I Became an Actual Writer

In early December of 2011, I embarked on a journey. It wasn't an exotic overseas vacation; more of a personal quest. I got in contact with an editor/publisher about developing a book. This would bring about the fruition of a dream, one that in my wildest imagination I didn't believe could or would come true.

I love to dream, and I like to dream big. I am most comfortable, however, with dreams that remain dreams, because dreams that come true bring change. Change can be scary. Don't misunderstand - I know change is inevitable. And that it can bring about life-altering changes for the better. The idea of better can paralyze you with fear, however.

As it turns out, my book got finished, and is now going to a second printing. I spent the week before the book launch in a complete state of panic. Fear almost rendered me immobile. When the day arrived, I was surrounded by friends and family. But I was still afraid. Every fiber of my being was yelling "Run and hide!"

I spend a lot of time in front of my computer. I am quite comfortable talking on the phone and having conversations with strangers - on a one-on-one basis. Large groups scare me; I try to avoid them.

At the book launch, I was expected to read aloud from my book. I stepped up to the podium and did what I had to do. My hands were shaking, and yet when I see pictures of the event now, I realize I used them when I spoke. The video is twelve minutes of me, reading, looking only a bit nervous. In the greater scheme of things in life, it seems silly. Yet it was so far out of my comfort zone, the reading seemed like 2 hours by the time it was finished.

When I think about that day now, I can't think of anything I would have changed. It was perfect. The people who love me were there. The support that surrounded me that day was inconceivable to me. I didn't run, throw up, or wet myself, and really those were the highest expectations I had. It's funny how God can surpass all of our expectations, even the ones we didn't know we had.

I don't know what happens from here. When I dreamed of publishing a book, before this year, I didn't dream about what would happen past the actual publication. I didn't even dream of telling anyone I had published a book. I think the main dream I had was that I would finish something that I had wanted to do, not for anyone else, but for me. The book is even available on all e-readers and the paperback is at the local Christian bookstore. That is far beyond any of my plans. The original idea was for me to have one print copy, and for my grandmother to have one. So the rest of it is all an additional blessing that my Father has given me.

I'm still worried about change. I'm a work in progress, what can I say? In my head, I enter negotiations with Him. Usually it goes like this:

- "OK, God. I realize that I don't know the full plan, but … if you could eliminate any public speaking from the plan, that would be great."
- "OK, God. I realize that I have to learn to fully rely on you and that you will never leave me nor forsake me, but… if you could make sure that I don't have to travel, that would be great."

Of course, if God were to call me to travel and speak in public again, I would go. Probably. I may not be comfortable with it, but He hasn't promised to never take me from my comfort zone.

I am very aware of the amount of growth that I still need to do. He is aware of my fear and that I prefer staying where I am. Maybe I am to go no farther than I have at this moment in time. I would be happy with that, and yet I wonder... if He has brought me this far, and I choose to not follow where He leads, what will I miss? Even though I am a scared and imperfect servant, what more could He use me for?

Getting Out of My Zone

When the comfort zone is no longer an option, then what?

I have been so comfortable. I cannot even put into words the comfort that I have in my comfort zone. When they say a man's house is his castle, I totally get it. I love my house.

I don't live in a mansion. I don't have maid service, I have a nice-sized house and I have kids (who sometimes do chores) and a husband (who sometimes does them too). I have three cats that don't use a litter box but all of the flower beds around my house instead. I have spots of grass from where we dumped things like oil or paint and it killed the grass. I have weeds that grow taller than my flowers. I have an office that will never be organized. Every spring, I get ants. The floors squeak upstairs in the bedrooms, there is a space in the hardwood floor in the front room.

None of this matters. I love every square inch of it. I even love the spiders that sometimes find a home in the corner of the bathroom. It's comfortable here, it's home.

When I am home, I watch television, I play games on the computer (FreeCell and Spider Solitaire are my favorites), I like to sing songs on the Sing It Game on the Wii. I like to go on bike rides with the kids, and take walks. I sometimes write. I go to a large church where I can blend in. I have friends there, but I would venture to say that there are far more that do not know me than do.

I talk to my friends at church before Sunday school and after but I never talk in class if I can help it. I go to Bible studies and I don't talk in class. I go to malls and make friends with the girls at the Clinique counter. I go to restaurants and make friends with the wait staff. I am really good at talking to strangers, and one on one. I am really good at talking to my friends, one on one. It's comfortable.

I enjoy working with children, but I don't want to teach; I want to be the aide. I decide what I will order at a restaurant once I see what others are ordering. I will go to Women of Faith this year, and I will be in awe of the women who can travel around and speak with such eloquence… but I don't want to be one of them. I would love go to lunch with them and have a conversation and be friends with any of them, but I don't want to do what they do.

I like my routine. I like knowing what's around the corner, that each day is not too much different than the day before. There are just different evening activities with the kids to go to. I forget things. I block things. I like to be comfortable, right here where I am, in my comfort zone.

But what if the comfort zone isn't an option? What if the call is to do more? How do you even know for sure what the call is? What if it's a wrong number? Seriously. I am a one-on-one girl. I am not a public speaker, even in a group of friends, much less in a group of people I don't know. I don't want to be on Oprah. I don't even know what station she is on now. I just want to be here, where it's comfortable, in my comfort zone.

I had to get up in front of people and speak once before. I cannot remember being more terrified. I don't want to repeat the experience. I survived it, sure, but the stress of it was painful. Well, I'm not sure if it was more painful for me or for those who had to endure listening to me. It's just not me. In Sunday school, we divide up in groups of men and women. In our groups we're given questions to answer. Recently, the questions were about comfort zones. I had, to this point, spoken during class exactly one time. That one time did not go so well, because I made a poorly-timed joke. If you do get my humor, it was pretty funny, but I realized immediately this was not the right crowd because everyone was looking at me like I had just grown three heads.

I haven't glimpsed the future, and I don't know what it holds. I only know that this fear consumes me. I feel as though I'm in a battle, and honestly, I'm tired. I am afraid that I'm going to be told to move and I don't have the right shoes. I don't have the compass, I haven't been given the map, I don't have a smart phone with GPS. I don't have that iPhone lady to tell me what I'm supposed to do. I'm not equipped and I'm not even sure I'm called. I don't even know how to tell if you are called, proving that I'm not equipped. People who are called are at least equipped enough to recognize the call, right?

If you get a call from God, how do you explain to the Creator of the Universe that you are the wrong gal? I know! It's crazy. God doesn't make mistakes. I know that. But does He not pay attention? Does He not realize that I'm just trying to blend in here?

I don't want to inspire anybody. I don't even necessarily want people to know I exist. Yet I wonder, when I die, if my family will sit around and tell stories about me to each other, because no one else will show up. I'm a blender-inner, not a stander outer. Blender inners don't inspire people to do anything. They just blend. They live, they hang out in their comfort zones and live their lives, and then they die. The end. That is MY plan. This plan will make for a smaller buffet at the funeral, I understand. It is my plan nonetheless.

But what if it isn't God's plan? What if He has another plan? What if I don't follow His plan, but follow my own? What if I do follow His plan, but He realizes I'm going to let Him down? How do you bounce back from that? These are all the crazy thoughts I keep having, and I don't even know if there IS a plan. Nope. I'm comfortable, right here where I am, in my comfort zone. Surely, that is where I'll stay. Don't you think?

Keeping up Appearances

I had a conversation recently with someone who was surprised to discover that I lack self-confidence. From her perspective, I seemed to have it all together. She was proved otherwise. I informed her simply because I know how to dress myself is not enough proof that I have anything together... other than my wardrobe.

This got me to thinking about how we are always trying to keep up with appearances. As if being real would be too much for others to handle. Like when we rush around and get the house picked up, if we find that someone is stopping by? How often do you go out in public without makeup on, and your hair done (assuming you are a woman, of course)?

<Tangent starting> If you are a man, well...I guess this doesn't really apply to you. Really, men have it made in this department. They get to wash, dry, dress, and go. There really isn't much to it. No makeup, very little hair product if any, AND they get to go grey. On them, it looks "distinguished." On women, it just makes us look old.

I have a friend (OK, it's me) that gets really anxious about people coming over. The house has to be perfect. She (again, me) is under the illusion that all of her friend's houses are perfect, all the time. They have it all figured out. They are all Martha Stewarts in training, or her understudies, and I am just flailing around trying not to catch the house on fire via the major appliances. She (yeah, me again) doesn't even iron clothes, and even avoids curling irons because she is THAT accident prone. Burn scars are not "in" at present. Sure their (our) clothes are sometimes wrinkled, but we have eaten enough fast food that we fill out our clothes nicely, which hides most wrinkles.

I sometimes even feel bad that our yard isn't sod, and that we haven't paid for professional landscaping. After all, I only have perfect people living around me, at least in my mind's imagination. I love the cartoon "The Family Circus," that shows all the toys in the yard and the kids running amok. The mom says they are growing "kids, not grass." What a great reminder. What is really important? Shouldn't we worry less about appearances and more about each other?

Shouldn't we accept ourselves just as Jesus has accepted us? How different would things be if we could accept ourselves as we are, not striving to be perfect, but simply to be what God intended for us? What if we threw the appearances rule book out the window? (Who would notice among the uncut grass and strewn sports equipment, anyway?)

One of the greatest joys in my life is when I get to relax and just be with my family or friends. If my house had to be perfect at all times, no one would ever be able to come over. Perfection eludes me, even when I think we have the house as clean as it is going to get. It's unattainable. And it's OK that it is.

As imperfect yet perfectly lovable people, loved by our God, we should be cherished by each other and not impressed. Romans 3:23 says, "For all have sinned and fall short of the glory of God." All have fallen short. There isn't a reason to impress God. No one would be able to fool God into thinking we were perfect. I don't think it matters as much what the neighbors think of us, as what God thinks.

That said, I should warn you that if you show up unannounced on a non-work day, around noon, I may still have my pajamas on. There were days over the last extended break from school that I didn't bother to dress at all, and spent the entire day in pajamas. I will also warn you that most of the time there is laundry in some form both in the laundry room and probably in the hallway. If I do manage to put clothes on, but I have nowhere to go, my favorite sweatpants have paint splattered all over them, and my hair will either look like I stuck my finger in a light socket or I will look like a boy, because it will be stuck to my head.

There. I can think of no other way to keep it real with you. I don't have it all figured out. I am not perfect. I am just trying to follow Jesus in everything I do. Jesus doesn't care about appearances; I don't think He expects perfection either. He expects obedience. If I can get that part worked out, I figure I'm good.

Coffee Shop or Library

One evening, I was invited to go to a local coffee shop to celebrate one of my friends' birthdays. Ten of us were there, gathered around a couple of tables pushed together, with coffee drinks, cheesecake and gifts. The birthday girl was one of the last to arrive, and stood in line to get her drink. While in line, one of the baristas told her to "remember that this is a coffee shop" and that we needed to "keep it down."

At which she replied, "Yes, but it isn't a library."

At this coffee shop, at any given time, you will find at minimum five college kids with laptops, working. While I understand the draw, at least half of the people that were with our party go to this coffee shop daily. A paying customer is a paying customer. And we weren't being particularly loud. We were just all chatting and laughing and having a good time. Not one person in our group was being inappropriate.

After several looks from the staff, we moved our party to the patio. There was one person on the patio working. It wasn't long before he packed up and moved inside. Of course, this sparked conversation amongst our group. The definition of a coffee shop according to The Free Dictionary online is: "A small restaurant in which coffee and light meals are served." It is a gathering place. Nowhere in the definition does it say you need to be quiet because college students may be studying.

I was once in college. We had dorm rooms, libraries, and student centers for studying. I have visited the college that these students attend. There is no shortage of places for them to study, especially since they all have their earbuds on, anyway.

A library has signs posted about being quiet, and librarians to tell you to be quiet. It is understood when you go into a library that you are to be quiet, as the place is full of books. Who reads well with noise? No one reads if it's noisy. Everyone reads in quiet; this is understood.

Who goes into a coffee shop and thinks "You know I should be quiet; this is a place for studying"? No one, that's who. One goes into a coffee shop with friends and thinks, "What a great place to share a drink and visit and enjoy time together." The music is nice, no one interrupts you, and very few of the other customers will be bothered, because they are plugged in. Worst case scenario is that they are IMing their friends to tell them that you are talking about periods and menopause and hair color. Or whatever it is you are getting together to talk about.

I was once kicked out of a bar for being too young. I was invited by some college classmates to go to lunch. I told them that I wasn't old enough to go to the place they chose, but they told me that you could go there just to eat lunch. They were wrong, and I was asked to leave. Apparently this establishment wasn't like a restaurant with a bar, it was like a bar that also served food. Good to know. I left, my classmates stayed and I went to a sandwich shop. Not a problem. They were right and I was wrong. Lesson learned. And it wasn't like I was trying to get away with anything—I was just trying to eat lunch.

This time, though, I was just trying to have coffee with friends and enjoy some time together, in a public domain that is not a library. I wouldn't go to a library and expect to be able to converse and laugh with friends. In a library, I would expect to be allowed to work on my computer, or read, or do research. I was not doing anything wrong or trying to get away with something that was uncouth.

There was one other adult there that was just having coffee and grading papers. While we were inside, she was cracking up.

At one point, she even leaned over and said that she appreciated the entertainment. I didn't see anyone going up to the counter to complain. So a collection of five women who are in Sunday school class together and another five people who run with the birthday girl were somehow too loud for a coffee shop.

I suppose next time we get together to celebrate at 8:30 p.m., we will have to choose another location. We are just too wild. Perhaps an ice cream parlor or another restaurant would be more suitable for our needs. Suggestions are appreciated.

Tim McGraw Day

We have some interesting conversations in the car.

Beginning in January this year, my husband, one of my daughters, and I began a quest to start eating healthier and trying to lose weight. We decided to try these diet shakes you have as a meal replacement for two meals a day. Then we weigh in once a month to check our progress. (As of the printing of this book, we have been off the shakes for a while, gained our weight back, and no longer find shakes very appealing.)

So after picking up the kids from school one day, I had the following conversation in the car.

Me: Guess what Friday is?

Daphne: "I've got the boom" day?

Me: No.

Megan: Mardi Gras?

Me: No.

Daphne: Tim McGraw Day!

Me: What is Tim McGraw day?

Daphne: You know, it's a day where everybody wears a Tim McGraw shirt and sings Tim McGraw songs!

Me: No! I don't even know any country songs. Friday is February 2.

Megan: No, Saturday is February 2.

Me: Oh. Then guess what Saturday is?

Daphne: What? What is the big deal about February 2?

Me: Weigh-in day!

Daphne: Wayans brothers' day?

Me: No! Weigh-in day!

Daphne: Oh…

She apparently wasn't as excited about weigh-in day as I was. Proving that I was in it to win it far more than she was, in our family friendly competition. (I lost in the end, by the way, and celebrated my loss with frozen yogurt).

But honestly, a Tim McGraw day? That's just silly. I don't even have snakeskin boots… anymore. And the only good country songs are from Garth Brooks from the early 1990s.

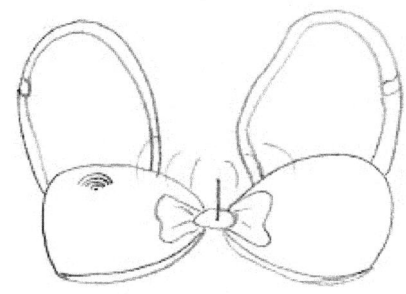

Why Is Underwear So Expensive If No One Ever Sees It?

Five pairs of underwear for twenty dollars, or is it four pairs for twenty-five? When did that become a good deal?

I walked into Victoria's Secret when I was bra shopping, and found one for over fifty dollars. Fifty dollars for a bra that no one but myself and perhaps my husband will see. Why? Are they gold plated? Was it once worn by a Greek Goddess? I don't understand. I cannot fully understand the need for a fifty-dollar bra.

Obviously, at my age, I am very concerned about having the best underwear one can buy... at Wal-Mart. If I am really going overboard, I will hit the clearance department at JCPenney. Honestly, it's spandex, lycra, and lace, maybe some foam for the push-up part. Why on earth do they cost so much, when they cover so little?

I am not a model; I don't want to be a model. I didn't even want to be a cheerleader when I was a kid because I thought the uniforms were inappropriate, and I was skinny then. My parts were all where they were supposed to be then. As you get older, things fall. But even a fifteen-dollar clearance bra from JCPenney will pick the girls up and pull them out of your navel.

I'm not sure who we are trying to impress here. It takes too much strategy to worry about lingerie. Maybe it's my age, or maybe it's the fact that I'm a mother, (other parents will get this) but when the opportunity arises to be well… intimate with my mate, I don't normally have time to go parading around in sexy lingerie. One of the kids might wake up, one of the kids may come home, or worse, into the room, or bang on the door … assuming you remembered to lock it. But then the mood is gone.

And when you have teenagers, they don't go right to sleep when they go to bed. If you shut the door before they are out, they know what is going to go down. My kids don't even like us to kiss or hug in front of them. I am not about to traumatize them for life and give them a runway show of me in my lingerie.

Perhaps I am missing something with the fifty-dollar bra. I am from a small town, so we have to drive to a big city to even see a Victoria's Secret store. Does the expensive bra permanently keep the girls in place? Is it so comfortable that you will want to sleep in it? Are the underwires such that they will never poke through and threaten to stab you in the heart? Is the foam memory foam, so the foam and the wire work together, signaling to each other that this is going to be harder work then they had anticipated, because unfortunately they didn't get purchased by a twenty-something who has parts still in place?

Is this bra so intelligent that it knows a forty-something who perhaps doesn't remember her natural hair color is wearing it, and the parts inside the bra cannot get up on their own? Does it come with wifi or its own hot spot, so your cell phone will work anywhere, as long as you are wearing the magical bra? Inquiring minds want to know.

I never really understood the need for expensive jeans either, until I tried on a pair of expensive jeans. I walked into this store, you know the ones, those that you usually just look in the windows and drool, wishing you weren't such a cheapskate so you could wear things from there? Well, one day I actually went in, and you know they convinced me to try on a pair of jeans. They said their jeans are the greatest things ever. I was very skeptical. I thought they must be crazy… until I tried them on.

These jeans have enough spandex in them that they fit everywhere properly. They don't cut off the circulation. They are fantastic. They make my other jeans look like tourniquets. I own one pair now, a birthday gift from my family. Not that I don't still wear my other jeans.

But I refuse to try on the bra. I will not get carried away. My mother was the biggest bargain shopper you would ever meet. What would she think? She didn't buy PopTarts without a coupon. Then again, she also had a QVC addiction, so we will just let the jeans thing slide.

A Lot Can Happen While in the Bathroom

It occurs to me that a lot can happen while one is in the bathroom. I do spend a great deal of time in the bathroom. Ordinarily, it is the quietest, most secluded room in my house. I always use the one attached to my bedroom. It is also warm in there with the door closed, because it is a very small room. If you have escaped to the bathroom to read, and have to, you know... go... you are already there.

However, allow me to introduce you to the things that happen when I am in the bathroom. I think you will understand why sometimes all you can do is hide in the bathroom and hope it all works out.

When my daughters were very young, and I needed a shower (and a few minutes of peace), they would be content watching one of their TV shows. One day, I went to take a shower before we were to leave to go out for lunch. While I was in the shower, my daughters informed me that there was a man at the door. I wasn't expecting my father to come to our house before meeting us for lunch, and was afraid they would open the door if I lingered in the shower, so I shut off the shower and put on a robe. With a towel on my head, I ran to the door to see who was there.

It was a man from the town inquiring about the shed being built in our backyard. It seemed that our shed was being built on top of the sewer line, and he wanted it moved promptly. I explained that I was obviously not in the position to move it right that very minute, and would take care of as soon as possible. He left and I went about getting myself ready.

Twenty minutes later, he was back. This continued every twenty minutes for more than an hour. The last time he came to my door, he actually commented that I was looking better. I informed him that with two small children and 20-minute increments to work with, that it was no small wonder I had gotten as far as I had.

My shed was the source of much stress for that day, from 10 a.m. till 7 p.m. By the end of the day I was ready to move away, even though we had just moved in three months before. For the record, the shed did get moved, and I still want to move, but only because I long for warmer temperatures.

Another time when I went to the restroom, the girls took crayons and colored all over the white walls in the family room. Red crayon. Big ovals. I had the stuff that was supposed to take the crayon off the wall. The only problem is that it leaves an oil mark on the wall you're trying to clean. We ended up painting the walls a wine color so that it wouldn't show up if they decided to do it again. (Did I mention we hadn't lived in the house very long at that point?)

As established previously, the girls are now teenagers. They are nineteen months apart. (No, I didn't realize what that would entail. I am an only child. I thought they would be best friends. Ha!) My first clue should have been a month after bringing the second baby girl home; the oldest wanted something from me while I was nursing the baby. I explained that I would get it as soon as I could, but she would have to wait. She got mad and hit her sister in the head. It hasn't stopped since.

I have a very sensitive, kind-hearted, loving little boy. He gets very upset when the girls fight. He comes running to inform me of these developments…and for some reason, these fights happen only when I am in the restroom. I think they plan their altercations around my visits to the restroom, actually. He will cry and want me to come right away to stop the fight. Finally, I started telling him that as long as no one was bleeding or on fire, I would finish my business and address them after that.

Isn't it interesting the things that can happen when one goes to the bathroom? You never go to the bathroom and come out to see that the dishes are done and the laundry is folded and put away. You don't go to the bathroom then come out to find that the kids decided to make you dinner. You don't go to the bathroom and find out you lost ten pounds, then get rewarded with a candy bar that takes off another five. If showering could wash away excess around the middle and chocolate was good for you... well, now I'm just fantasizing.

A lot can happen when one goes to the bathroom. I have a friend that walked in to use the bathroom and her water broke. Everything worked out; she had a beautiful little girl. But you get how sometimes just going to the bathroom can take your life in a different turn.

Isn't that how life is sometimes? You can be going about your regular day and all of a sudden something can change. A sunrise or sunset will take you in by its beauty. A job will change, a dinner will turn out, a baby will be born; any number of things can happen. God is full of mysteries and joy can be found in the unexpected, even when you go to the bathroom. Or maybe, when you come out of the bathroom.

The Urologist's Office

The setting: the urologist's office. We showed up for an appointment roughly 20 minutes late. I am there, with three kids in tow. When I signed in, the receptionist asked me if I was aware that the appointment was at 3:15 p.m. I said I was aware, and like my husband informed her the previous day, we would be a few minutes late, but would be there as soon as we could get there after picking the kids up from school. She scowled.

There were other patients waiting, so it was obvious we weren't causing that big of a problem. They weren't exactly sitting around twiddling their thumbs, awaiting our arrival. I have yet to enter that office and been taken straight back. I am fine with this, because they have fantastic magazines. I enjoy the Reader's Digest.

We sit and we wait. By the time we are taken back and placed in our room (after weighing in and other preliminaries), it is after 4:00 p.m.

They have educational posters in a urologist's office. The one on the back of the door in the room was of prostate cancer. So you can imagine the conversation that took place.

Daphne: Prostate cancer? Do I have a prostate?

Me: No, you are a girl.

Daphne: Oh... cool.

Scotty: Do I have a prostate then, since I am a boy?

Me: Yes.

Scotty: Well, where is it?

Megan: It's in your penis.

Me: Megan!

Megan: Well, it is.

Me: Not exactly.

Daphne: No, it's not!

Scotty: Well, where is it then?

Me: It's... well... it's in a location that you can discuss with your father. That is a daddy question.

Scotty: Oh.

Daphne: What's wrong, mom, are you uncomfortable?

Megan: Yeah, mom, what's wrong? Still traumatized from having to teach me how to use a tampon?

Me: Yes! I am still traumatized from that and I don't wish to get into this here.

Scotty, looking around the room: What is lubricating gel?

Me, groaning: Nothing you need to concern yourself with. Please sit down and read your book.

At last, the doctor comes in and we have our conversation.

As we are getting into the car a few minutes later, Daphne finds a lighter on the ground. She picks it up and says, "Hey mom, look what I found." I make her throw it back down and give her hand sanitizer.

It is times like these that I am pretty sure that I was given wolves to raise. I know I told them about picking things up off the ground. It may have been along with the stranger danger talk. They don't talk to strangers, so at least I'm halfway there.

Unwanted Visitors

Both of my girls having their monthly visitors at the same time would seem like a gift, if it wasn't. It would be nice to have one of them stable, while the other one is off kilter. They bicker, and then they come up with the oddest conversations. This is a representative conversation in the car on the way to school:

Me: Does everyone have what they need? Do you two have extra "supplies" to get through the day?

Girls: Yes mom, we're good.

Me: OK. Just keep your mouths shut and I think you can get through the day without getting into trouble.

Megan: But what if someone comes up to me in the hallway and punches me in the face?

Me: What? Why would someone do that?

Megan: I don't know. But they could, so what then?

Me: Then you don't retaliate. You go to the office and tell them that someone just punched you in the face, and that your mom said that if that ever happened, you were not allowed to retaliate. Tell them and they will take care of it.

Megan: What if they don't?

Me: Then tell them that, at present, both you and your sister have your monthly bills, and that means that your mother is right behind you, so she is premenstrual. If they think you two are scary, they haven't seen anything yet. Your mom makes Helena Bonham Carter characters look like church mice, and she will be in the office to have a "chat."

<I am not sure why they start laughing at that statement. But then...>

Daphne: You are so great. <between giggles> Helena Bonham Carter... that is so funny.

Me: Does everyone feel better now? Can you get out of my car and go to school? Because I have to get to work.

Girls: Yes, mom.

Me: OK, I love you. Have a great day, God be with you.

Girls: With you too, bye. Love you.

<They get out of the car and we start pulling out of the parking lot when...>

Scotty: Church mice, huh?

Me: I guess. Either way, they got out of the car right?

Scotty: (pause) So we are having "the talk" today in school.

Me: Yeah?

Scotty: Yeah.

Me: Well, good luck with that. Be glad you are a boy.

Scotty: Every day.

Section 2

Dear Mom,

It has been nine years since you went home to be with Jesus. It is hard to believe that next year will be ten years. It seems surreal to me that you are gone, yet life continued. So much has happened. I am sure that you probably know everything because you get filled in up there, or you're allowed to find out for yourself. But here is the lowdown, just in case you have been too busy to check.

Daphne is now a licensed driver. She will be a senior this year and I am fearful of what she will eat when she graduates from college, because currently she only knows how to fix frozen pizza. I don't worry about while she is in college, because we have visited several colleges now, and they offer cooked food there. What will she survive on, if the only thing I've taught her to cook is frozen pizza? Epic fail on my part.

Megan has her driver's permit, but I'm too big a chicken to let her drive me around. I guess I feel about driving the way you felt about sex ed. It's best left up to the professionals. We have had several talks with them about sex, drugs, and rock and roll. I just have a fear of having them drive me. Also, I may have failed at teaching them both to cook, and to reapply sunscreen. It is entirely possible that I sheltered them so much they may live with me forever. I will have built-in house sitters forever when Vaughn and I want to travel. But I digress....

Scotty is growing up. He brings balance to our home. He has a lot of his dad in him. They both have a calming quality to them. He went to camp for the first time this year. We missed him so much. Our little peacemaker had the time of his life in the great outdoors, and cannot wait to go back next year. I'm pretty sure that he has decided he loves camp more than he loves baseball. He doesn't want to miss it again now that he has experienced it. (Much the way I feel about the Women of Faith conference. .) He is so smart and so kind. You would have really enjoyed getting to know the boy we were both nervous about.

I have made mistakes, but I have gotten a few things right too. They are all great swimmers and so brave. They amaze me with the things they have been able to do. They are so unique. Each one of them so different. I thought being raised in the same family, under the same roof, would make them similar. They are also very funny, and they have such big dreams.

I can't wait to see how they all turn out. Truth be known, I'm hoping that I haven't messed them up too much, and that they will succeed in spite of me.

I'm working on another book hope to have it out soon. I would like to try my hand at fiction, but I can't seem to find the time when the kids keep giving me so much new material. (Every time I sit down to write, the kids take turns asking me questions and distracting me. It's like when I get on the phone. If I don't do anything, they ignore me. Once I attempt to accomplish something, suddenly I'm the most interesting thing in their world. Did I do that to you?)

I am also working with kindergarteners again this year. I love that age. They are so eager to learn and they say the funniest things. Their eyes shine when they learn something new. I have also loved getting to know all of the people I work with. I have made some new friends, and for that I am thankful.

Vaughn is still working hard to keep food on the table and a roof over our heads. He really is the most amazing husband and father. I am very blessed. We are dreaming of the future and enjoying the moment. He makes me a better me. He takes me out of my comfort zone on occasion. He has me try things I am afraid of, yet protects me at the same time. I may not experience life and all it has to offer if it weren't for him. He helps me live even when life seems overwhelming and I just want to hide. I hope we get to grow old and grey together and feed each other oatmeal.

I think that wraps it all up for a little while. Except that my birthday will be celebrated on January 15 from now on, instead of July 15. Now we can see who has the blizzard on her birthday, me or you. I probably won't get away with it and will be forced to keep celebrating my actual birthday, but it would be nice to be able to switch to a much less stressful and emotional time of year.

As always, I miss you and long for the day that Jesus comes to take us home so we can all be together again. I long to be at home in my Father's house. I hope to be fulfilling His work, so that one day He will tell me "Well done, good and faithful servant."

I hope this letter finds you and you know that although you are gone, you are still loved and not forgotten. You continue to live in my heart. If you could send me a message once in awhile, especially when I'm attempting to cook, my family would thank you.

Love always,

Heather

Question:
What Are You Doing With Your One and Only Life?

"What are you doing with your one and only life?"

This question, posed in the movie "Won't Back Down," really stuck with me. I'm not sure why. Most of the time I really have no idea what I'm doing. I have no real plan.

I tend to fly by the seat of my pants. I have a calendar that I sometimes check. I know where I am Monday through Friday from 7:45 to 12:50. I know where the kids are from 7:45 to 3:00. I have to check the calendar for my husband's schedule (he isn't a 9-to-5 kind of guy; his is a three-week rotating schedule, and I rarely know which week he's on). I tend to know the day of the week, but not the date. I am good at making lunch plans, but I don't really plan much past that.

What are you going to do with your one and only life? Wow. It's kind of a loaded question, isn't it? Part of me thinks, "Haven't I done enough?" The other part of me thinks, "Don't I have everlasting life to look forward to?"

How much is it acceptable to accomplish? When do I get to say "I'm accomplished"? Does that ever happen? Do people say that about themselves and I have just never heard it? Do people talk about others and describe them as "accomplished"? I don't think I have ever said that about someone before. My mind doesn't go there. I don't think to myself, "Wow, look how accomplished Sally is." I suppose I should look at what it means to be accomplished.

The Merriam-Webster Dictionary defines accomplished as:

> 1 *a* : proficient as the result of practice or training <an *accomplished* dancer>; *also*: skillfully done or produced <an *accomplished* film> *b* : having many social accomplishments.
>
> 2 : established beyond doubt or dispute <an *accomplished* fact> Synonyms for accomplished are: Cultivated, civilized, couth, cultured, genteel, polished, refined.

Hmm. Being accomplished may be out of my reach. I live in a small town and I don't get out much. The only cultivating happening around here is in the fields around my house. I am civilized mostly, unless you happen to be in my car while I'm dancing and singing. Couth is a word I don't use at all, so I don't think I am sophisticated. Cultured? Not unless it counts that I know which fork to use. Genteel, OK. Polished? All except for my nails. Refined, no. I'm still in the refining process.

I can't be accomplished because I'm not a diamond. I'm not even a diamond in the rough. I am charcoal. I'm still being refined. It might be about 15,000 years before I get there. The day I get to Heaven, I will be accomplished.

Before Heaven, I think we just keep working towards… well, getting to be with God. Isn't that the ultimate goal? Do the things of this world, or rather, society's definition of accomplishment, really matter?

Micah 6:8: "What does the Lord require of you? To act justly and to love mercy and to walk humbly with your God."

If we could do all of that, we could say we've met the ultimate goal. Perhaps when we get that figured out, we can *be* accomplished. Until then, we just keep getting our charcoal pressed, by the Ultimate Craftsman.

What Are You Waiting For? GO!

This summer was the summer of waiting. In October, we hired someone to build a new deck by our pool. Our old deck had been built by my husband and me, close to ten years ago. It had seen better days, especially considering we didn't know what we were doing.

My husband and one of our friends spent a rainy Saturday in October taking apart the old deck and hauling it away. We then told our deck guy we were ready... and we waited. Apparently the time frame for getting a deck done is nine months. Had I been a younger gal, I would have gotten pregnant, and we could have raced to see who got to the finish line first.

Our deck was finally ready, in time for our Fourth of July party. However, the pool heater that we have been waiting to get fixed was not fixed, and will not be. It now must be replaced. At the middle point of a rainy Midwestern summer, that can wait until next year. We also waited two weeks for our air conditioner to get fixed.

Now we are waiting to go on vacation. This summer tried our patience with all of the waiting for things that we had hoped would make this a great summer.

In thinking about this summer of waiting, I have been thinking about waiting in other areas of life as well. We wait to meet the right partner to share our lives with. We wait nine months for a baby (or a deck, apparently). We wait for school to end and our lives to begin. We wait for vacations. We wait for seating at restaurants. We wait in line to ride rides. We wait for movies. We wait for books. We wait.

That is a lot of time waiting for things, some that matter and some that don't. I have spent much of my summer frustrated and waiting for things to be accomplished. I could have spent that time in a much better way. For that, I am sorry.

Spending all of your time waiting is a waste of time. What could you do if you weren't waiting? Personally, the only thing I want to wait for is for Jesus. And I don't want to spend so much time waiting, that I don't spend it living. You can spend time worrying and waiting for things to change in the world around you… or you can be the change you want to see. It is a choice. You know what happens when you wait? Life happens, and you could miss out on things you could have done and places you could have seen, and people you could have spent time with. You know what else? Waiting is boring.

I have wanted to put some funky color in my hair for years. I never did it before, because I have daughters who would throw a fit every time I talked about it. I have wanted some cool plastic-framed glasses, but everyone else likes the wire frames better on me. I wanted to try archery just because I wanted to see if I could be like Katniss Everdeen in "The Hunger Games" or Mia from "The Princess Diaries 2." I talked myself out of doing these things, because I think I'm too old. I should sit back, because it is my childrens' turn and not mine. My time has come and gone.

You know what that is? A big bunch of fear, and crap.

Today, I had just a few bright red highlights put in my hair. The eye place ordered the wrong glasses by mistake, so I got the plastic frames I had wanted in the first place. This summer, my daughter and I went to a garage sale at my friend's house, and her husband taught us how to shoot a bow and arrow.

What am I teaching my children, if I don't do things because they (and I) think I'm old? That when you get old, you don't get to dream, or live? What kind of message is that? If I want my children to spend their lives not only dreaming, but chasing their dreams and trying new things, I have to be willing to do that myself. If not, the only thing I am teaching them is to give up.

If I truly believe in God and his teachings then I have to believe that even if I can't do something then I can do it with his help. How awesome and reassuring is that, when it comes to pursuing dreams that God has placed in your heart to begin with?

I'm middle aged now. I need to get busy before my time really does run out. So get going already! In the words of Ferris Bueller, "Why are you still here? It's over. Go!"

My Son's Multiple Careers: Preacher, Masseur, and… Stripper?

My son has a great faith, and has been dubbed the peacemaker in our house. My grandmother thinks he is going to grow up to be a preacher or a missionary. He has been known to be the mediator among his friends, and also to minister to them when they are angry. He may very well grow up to be a minister; I don't know.

Scotty also has decided he likes to give massages. My back was bothering me and he offered to rub my back. I thought this was very sweet of him to want his mother to feel better. That is until he told me that it was going to cost me five dollars. I just looked at him.

I then said, "OK, well, dinner tonight is going to cost you five dollars for your food. So we will call it even." My massage came to an abrupt stop. Now he will massage just about anyone, if they are in pain or not. Of course a great deal of his "massaging" is him pounding on your back, so it may be just a way for him to pound on people without getting into trouble. The idea of my son becoming a preacher is a nice one. A masseur… eh, maybe he will need to work on his delivery.

Why did I mention that he could be a stripper? The problem is that his clean laundry will be downstairs, because he has not taken it up to put it away. So he will come downstairs in his underwear in the morning, looking for clothes. Then half the time when I tell him in the evening to go upstairs to take a shower and get ready for bed, he will come into the room I am sitting in and shake his booty at me while he is in his underwear.

After his shower, if I go upstairs to check on him, he will be in his room with the door wide open, and he will shake his naked booty at anyone passing by. The boy is not at all modest. We have had to talk to him about not walking in on others when they are changing. If a door is closed, it is closed for a reason. We are also discussing his closing his own door.

Whatever Scotty decides to do, he will do it with passion and love. My boy has Jesus in his heart. While he does like underwear time, I think he's just confident. Imagine if we could be so happy with what we saw in the mirror!

Maybe he will be a preacher, or a masseuse, or a doctor, or a world-traveling scientist. No matter what, I will be proud of the man of God he is growing up to be.

You Might Have a Little Teeny Tiny Bit of Road Rage If…

I am not particularly fond of driving. Part of the reason for that is that I am pretty sure that when I am driving, I should be the only one on the road. Motorcycles scare me and teenage drivers scare me.

Yes, I realize I was once a teenage driver, and I will apologize for that. I actually got into a wreck because I wasn't watching where I was going. I was very busy trying to find a new station on the radio, but I believe that that is why God now put the station changer on my steering wheel, so I don't have those distractions anymore.

But now, even if the teenage drivers have that button on the wheel for changing the station, we also have to tweet that we are leaving school and post at least six Facebook updates to make sure everyone knows we are "getting a coke zero at the gas station because we are having an OK day." (Easy A reference. I'm pretty sure this earns me bonus "cool" points with the teenagers.) But it isn't just the teenagers; it's their parents too.

I have two at the high school, and I have to take them. Yesterday while driving to school, it went like this.

I pull up at the light and am ready to turn, but I have to wait, as there are children walking across the road. It is twenty-three degrees, so maybe their blood has frozen, because they are in no hurry to get across the road. So I say, "Seriously? Pick up bricks, kids! It is not a marathon getting across the street. It's a race, and cars are coming. Move it, move it, move it!"

They couldn't hear me of course, because it was twenty-three degrees outside and my windows were up. But my kids heard me.

It gets better. I finally get to the high school and there is a minivan taking up residence in front of the door. The kid gets out of the van and walks into the school, and yet the van stays put. No other kids get out. Then it occurs to me that they are waiting for the kid to get through both sets of doors. Really? Both sets of doors?

At that point, I have this reaction: "Are you serious, Avon? Really? You drove them here. Where are they going to go? Do you need to park and hold their hand and make sure they go potty? It's high school! Move!" So finally Avon moves on and my kids get out and walk to the doors. I do not wait to see if they made it. I move on.

It is not easy to get out of the parking lot. I pull up to the stop sign to leave the high school, and there is one car in front of me. There are no cars coming from the right, and one car that is clearly turning, coming from the left. The car in front of me is going to turn right, but refuses to move. The heavens have to be perfectly aligned to have this scenario happen, to get us out of the high school parking lot so easily. Usually it takes forever. But that day it was all aligned and this car refuses to go. So I say, "Good grief! Do you need a written invitation? Just GO! They are turning! Move! I have places to go. Some of us have to go to work." The car finally moves and we get out onto the road.

Today, I dropped the girls off without incident. Didn't have any yelling at other drivers to do until… I pull away from the front of the school, when I see a car barreling through the parking lot, headed our way. I slow down to a crawl and say, "Are you serious! There is a storm coming, so you think you need to get here as fast as you can? You are in a parking lot, you nutball! Slow down! We are not going to die today because you refuse to use any sense whatsoever and act like an idiot!"

Then I had to eat some humble pie. I got to the road and my ten-year-old, who had been listening to me yell at other drivers for two days, says, "Um, wow, mom! You might have some road rage issues to work out. Calm down!"

I told him that maybe I should write about my road rage. He said he thought that was a good idea. Then I told him, "Well, Scotty, I think we really need to pray for the idiot drivers, because they are giving me high blood pressure!"

He said, "Yeah, ok." But I think he is going to pray for me instead.

Maybe the teenagers come by their overly dramatic antics honestly. Maybe a premenstrual woman shouldn't be allowed to drive in high school parking lots. Maybe I, as Megan would say, just need to "calm the heck down." I do need to be a bit more accepting.

I have been quite exasperating to my friends and family of late, for many reasons. I tend to get worked up over things that I have little or no control over. I cannot control the driving of other drivers. I can only keep my children safe when I am behind the wheel.

I cannot control what God has planned for me, even if I am terrified of what I think his plan is. To be clear, it isn't that I don't trust God, I don't trust myself. I am also far better at giving pep talks and building other people up than I am at doing that for myself. I have an "I can't" attitude, unless it comes to driving. Then I do that better than the others in the high school parking lot.

The Best You Can Be

What if it isn't a matter of trying to be something we are not, but rather a matter of trying to be something we could be? Something we *should* be. What if we weren't trying so hard to run away from something, but rather running towards something? Something better.

These are the questions that are ruminating in my mind. "Therefore, if anyone is in Christ, he is a new creation; the old has gone, the new has come!" That verse from 2 Corinthians 5:17 is what I keep coming back to. The fact is that I am trying, with the help of my God, to be the new creation that He has in mind for me to be. I am not interested in running away from anything anymore. I'm more interested in running towards what I could be; something better than what I once was.

The idea of that is scary. While I know that I am forgiven, and that God has a big plan for me, I can't understand why He would choose me. I would never choose me. I can think of at least five people I would choose over me.

I am very content with life as it is right now. I am married to the best guy, I have three great kids, and I enjoy being in my house to the extent that I no longer have to be constantly moving. I like it here. I have friends here, and I have a job I love. This is home. But am I being the best I can be?

Am I fulfilling what God has planned for me? What if there is something more? How do you adjust your thinking when you are already happy with your life? How do you say "OK, God, your plan is better than my plan, I'm ready to go from good to better"? I don't know how to do that. I mean, I'm a mess, but I'm not as big of a mess as I used to be. Apparently God has more up his sleeves for me. Maybe He has more up his sleeves for you, too.

One of my favorite verses is Jeremiah 29:11: " 'For I know the plans I have for you' declares the Lord,' plans to prosper you and not to harm you, plans to give you hope and a future.'" He knows his plans for us. We don't necessarily know, but we have to trust His plans.

So that is what I'm working on. I have trust issues but I'm learning that where I come from and where I have taken myself don't have to define me. Only God can define me. I just have to get out of my own way - God has this one under control.

WebMD, Go Away!

Daphne may be a hypochondriac, and I blame WebMD and "Boy Meets World." Sure that sounds crazy, but it's true. She loves the show "Boy Meets World," and on that show, Cory was a hypochondriac in at least one episode. I have thought her personality was very much like his. I just didn't expect her to come to me one day and say, "Mom, I think you should know that I have Mad Cow Disease."

Mad Cow Disease... really? Who just out of nowhere thinks they have Mad Cow Disease? The kind of people who spend time plugging symptoms into WebMD trying to self-diagnose and find out what is wrong with them, that's who.

I said to her, "Really? You think you have Mad Cow Disease? Why?" She said that was what WebMD told her. I then asked her when was the last time she remembered having red meat. We eat a LOT of chicken. So I told her, "Maybe you have Mad Chicken Disease."

Her face actually lit up. "Yes, that must be it. Is that a thing?"

"No, I made it up." A nurse practitioner even told her that there hadn't been a case of Mad Cow in the US that she knew of since 2003. Thanks WebMD.

It has gotten a little crazy. She also isn't pregnant, doesn't have hepatitis, and she doesn't have a staph infection. Next, she will be coming to tell me that she has prostate cancer, and I will have to tell her that she doesn't have a prostate. Of course, there is an app for WebMD, and she has it. WebMD is definitely not for teenagers, so I have told her to stay off it.

I am sure there is a use for this site, but my teenage daughter doesn't need it. There should be apps specific to teenagers. Make study tools as apps, and maybe they would use them. Perhaps she should have an app for algebra, or an app for driving, or an app for science. Those would actually be helpful.

She is healthy, she is young, and she is just fine. Fortunately, she got a job for the summer. Unless she hates her job, she will not have any time to spend trying to figure out what is wrong with her. I suppose one day she will tell me she has Mad Teenager Disease. Now that would be believable.

Who's Driving the Boat?

I had a dream last night that I was driving down the road, and there was water on the road. Along the way, there appeared a boy who was driving a boat down the road. I called him Jimmy, and asked him what he thought of all the water on the road. He said he wasn't concerned because he had a boat, and that he would travel beside me in case I needed to get in.

When I woke up, I actually looked outside to see if there was water on the road. The driveway was a bit wet, like it had rained, but I didn't see any standing water. I was relieved, because I don't know anyone named Jimmy that has a small wooden boat that can travel on dry land AND water.

What is interesting about this dream is that I remembered it. Usually, if I remember the dream when I wake up, it is gone by the time my feet hit the floor. I am not a dream interpreter, but I would venture a guess as to what this dream was telling me. I remember thinking that if the water were to continue to rise, I might be in some trouble. Jimmy seemed as though we were friends and that he was there to help me.

I have felt very overwhelmed lately. I think perhaps the dream was a reminder. Not that I shouldn't drive when there is water rising on the road — that part I get — but maybe it's a reminder that I should know that I'm not alone. Maybe I don't have any actual friends named Jimmy, who owns a boat to travel with me when the water gets too deep. I have something better.

I have someone who is always there. Someone who is traveling the road of life beside me, who loves me, who wants me to grow into something beautiful; who, when the water rises, can calm the roughest seas. I have a Heavenly Father. I have a boat. I just have to remember who the Captain is, and it's not me. This is a good thing, because I can't pilot a boat. I would run it aground. It's hard not being able to see a map, to see where the boat is going, but even if I were privy to that information, it probably wouldn't help my anxiety. It might even make it worse. I also think it would defeat the purpose. How do you grow if you already know the plan? How do you learn to trust, if you can see what lies ahead?

I don't know if that is the proper analysis of my dream or not. Maybe it was just raining and my subconscious was messing with me. Maybe I've read too many jokes about a boy named Jimmy. I'm not sure. I can still see the dream as clearly now as I did when I dreamed it. I feel better knowing that even if I'm wrong, I think the interpretation is something more than a boy and a boat. It's about my lifeline still being intact, my Redeemer still being the captain, and I'm just along for the ride. Even if it comes to an end, it was quite a ride. It was mine, unique and special. That is good enough for me.

Cheeseburgers

When I was pregnant with my first child, I had cravings for cheeseburgers. We would stop and pick up a double cheeseburger at one end of town, and by the time we got to the other end of town, I would want another one. I have not actually craved a cheeseburger since. Until recently, when we started drinking shakes to lose weight.

Sixty days in and the shakes, while they are not bad tasting, are getting old. I started thinking about what would make them better. If I could eat a cheeseburger while I drink the shake, it would make the shake taste better. Cheeseburgers are also warm, so I wouldn't get so cold while having my shake.

I actually called it my "stupid" shake recently, because I seem to have plateaued and don't seem to be losing the weight anymore. My husband was shocked the first time I called them that, as he has been successful with them. I informed him that when the scales started moving again, they would stop being stupid.

This spawned the following conversation with my husband, in the car:

Me: I think that the shakes have stopped working for me.

Vaughn: Why do you think that?

Me: Because I haven't lost any weight in weeks. Also, I think they would be better if I could eat a cheeseburger with it.

Vaughn: A cheeseburger?

Me: Yes, because shakes and cheeseburgers go together.

Vaughn: Wouldn't that defeat the purpose of the shake?

Me: If it were a good shake, it would counterbalance the cheeseburger and it wouldn't matter. Besides, no one says "Hey, I am having a shake! What would taste good with that? Oh, I know: a salad!" It's just not done. Cheeseburgers and shakes go together.

Vaughn: I think you need to give it more time to work.

Me: I will, but I don't have to like it. And if I don't lose at least twenty-five pounds at the end of this nonsense, I'm switching to something else.

Vaughn: That's fine. What is it with you and cheeseburgers lately?

Me: I have no idea. I think it's the shakes.

Part of what drew me to this shake program we are on is that you can eat what you want for one meal a day. You just have to drink the shakes for two meals. But drinking that many shakes makes you crave cheeseburgers, even if there's no chance of your being pregnant.

I mentioned on Facebook how great a cheeseburger would be, and one of my friends ended up sending her daughter to deliver me a cheeseburger. A cheeseburger never tasted so good. But I didn't drink a shake with it. Who had time to make a diet shake when it was the one meal a day that I get to eat solid food? Not me, I tell you! I savored every bite of that cheeseburger and wished I had another one.

I know that diet and exercise are important, but I also think that depriving yourself of the things you enjoy will set you up for failure. If someone said I have to work out every day (or at all really), AND give up all of the foods I love, I don't think that I would succeed.

By the way, it's worse to be on the shake diet, after you actually do eat a cheeseburger.

I'm not sure if this shake idea is really any better than eating a couple of rice cakes with peanut butter for breakfast and a cup of coffee with fat-free creamer… but then again, I can do anything for ninety days.

Was That a Burp or is a Large Truck Stopping Outside?

My goodness! What was that sound? Did that sound really come from me? That even startled me. The kids and the cats looked at me in disbelief.

"Wow, was that a truck?" I say. I even go to the window to look outside. Of course, there aren't any trucks on our little road. Jinkies. That was to be my out.

I have been belching. I'm not sure what to attribute this new development to. I have been crunching on a lot of ice, but I'm not sure that would cause it. It wouldn't be so bad if it wasn't so loud. Fortunately, I have it under control when out in public. But when we're in the car, it is especially bad. I have started calling the car our "safe place" for bodily functions, at least, ones that aren't messy. Need to belch? Go ahead. Need to pass gas? Go ahead! We have power windows, after all.

It does help having the "safe place" now. The others aren't allowed to complain in the safe place, unless it is done with ill intent. If they claim ill intent, then we will have to enter into "safe place" court and they can plead their case. That has never happened, so I'm not sure what would happen after that. It's not something one can control necessarily.

This isn't even something I can pass off as a skill set. I do love to sing. I could try to develop this into a musical, albeit disgusting, talent. But I can't even belch my ABC's. What good is it if you can't belch the ABC's or some other song? I just don't have the time to learn that. In my line of work (being a wife/mom/teacher's aide/kid runner/laundress/chef/housekeeper/vacation planner/procrastinator/writer, or WMTAKRLCHVPPW for short, that's what we in the biz call it), I have to talk to people. Not all at the same time, of course, but I cannot very well be having a discussion with someone and belch in their face mid-sentence. It is considered rude in most (OK, all, I think) cultures.

If this keeps up, I may need to find a support group. (There are support groups for a lot of things these days. I'm not sure what that is about. When I was growing up, if you had a problem, you just had to get over it. There weren't any support groups for talking about your feelings.)

Imagine what the meetings would be like: people sitting around, taking turns standing up and saying something like, "Hello, My name is Heather and I'm a belcher."

"Hello Heather!"

"Hi! Thanks everyone. I've been a belcher for six months." The moderator would thank everyone for coming and tell them that after the meeting there are sodas and chips and cheese in the back of the room, if you are interested in refreshments. Maybe not.

I went onto Google to look it up. Actually, I looked up menopause, because I thought it could be a symptom. I haven't anyone to ask about these things, remember? I tried to steer away from the WebMD site, because if I go there, I will discover that it could be at least six life-threatening diseases, and I should see a medical professional ASAP. I have no time for that. Isn't it funny how it's always something so serious when you go there? Want to scare a hypochondriac into straightening out? Send them to WebMD. They will either be convinced they are dying of Bird Flu or Mad Cow, or they will get over themselves already.

I don't remember what it said I had. I just bought some antacids and decided to move on. But if you ride in my car during one of my episodes, I apologize in advance.

Christmas Reflections

This time of year, I do a lot of reflecting. Memories flood my mind like a monsoon. Some make me smile; others make me cry. Christmas being what it is, a time to celebrate the coming of the Christ child, is the appropriate time to do just that.

The tree always stood in front of the window in the living room. It is funny; I cannot remember a single special ornament, or what we put on the top of the tree. I remember every year when I was old enough to figure it out, I would go into the living room and carefully unwrap each item in my stocking. I would then rewrap them and place them carefully back into the stocking and wait. And I had to wait until a certain time to wake up my mother on Christmas morning. The one year she had to wake me up, she was disappointed.

The entire family would go to grandma's house on Christmas morning. No less than twenty people piled into her small house that day. I remember every inch of that house. I remember the look of every room, the pictures that hung on the walls, the furniture, the position of the furniture in every room. The haze of smoke that hung in the air. If I close my eyes, I can see each family member in the rooms they would gravitate to.

The food for our feast would cover the counters and the table, and desserts would be on top of the chest freezer just outside the kitchen. We always had green bean casserole. I'm not sure who made it. And one of my aunts made the best yeast rolls. I remember that we thought she worked so hard on them, and they ended up being from a package.

The house is no longer standing anymore. It was torn down several years ago and now it is an empty lot.

Where once I didn't have a Sunday or a holiday without all of them, now I see the few remaining relatives just at funerals; but not a card or phone call during the year. I still see two family members from my mother's side at Christmas time; my cousin and her daughter. It is the highlight of the season for me. For those few hours, I am taken back to a time that helped to form and shape who I would become. I am the oldest cousin again. We tell lots of stories and catch up on what we have missed.

We tell our kids about the pink flamingo and blue ribbon clubs; clubs we made up, of course. We used my grandmother's dryer sheets to make blue ribbons. For the pink flamingo, you would have to ask my cousin. I no longer remember anything but the name. We tell them how my cousin would read the Reader's Digest, and how I would beg her to hurry up and finish reading so we could play.

When your matriarch is gone, and her daughters are gone, who holds a family together? If you know a family that has succeeded in holding itself together, I would be interested in knowing how it's done. It makes me incredibly sad and I miss my mother so much it takes my breath away.

With Christmas approaching, I think of those times with bittersweet memories, and yet I look around at all I have been given, and my tears turn to joy, because I know the Lord had a hand in making it all happen. You see, my family didn't go to church. The only churches I entered as a child were those of my friends. I only remember my mother going to church for four events before she was diagnosed with cancer: my wedding and the baptism of my three children.

While I miss my mother every single day, I wonder if she had lived longer, if she would have come to know Christ as her Savior. I don't know if she would have been baptized, and been able to walk the streets of gold. If there is anything I can say that could be good about cancer it is this: my mother did come to know Christ before she passed. I will see her again, because I know without a doubt she is in Heaven. If she had never gotten sick, but had been hit by a bus or some other tragedy had struck her down early instead, I don't know that she would be there.

My mother will be spending her ninth Christmas with Jesus this year. I have to say, I am a bit jealous. Don't get me wrong -- I love every inch of my life. I love my husband, my children, my home, my family, my friends, my friends who are like family, and even my three crazy cats. But how glorious would it be to spend Christmas, the day we celebrate the birth of our Lord Jesus, with the man himself? (Don't worry, I have no plans of going anywhere soon. I just no longer have a fear of what comes next after this life. While this life is pretty good, it's not near as good as what is waiting for me.)

This year, as you light your tree, and take the pictures of the kids opening their gifts from Santa, I would like to challenge you to not only remember those times when you were a child, but also to remember the reason we celebrate in the first place.

And if you are missing someone like I am, it's OK. When you say your prayers thanking God for his Son, He doesn't get mad if you ask him to tell them you miss them. He understands our humanness and loves us. Don't get so caught up in Santa and shopping that you forget to share the memories, and share the reason.

The End of the World As We Know It
(Diary entry: December 22, 2012)

According to the Mayan calendar, I shouldn't be typing on my computer today. The end of the world should have happened yesterday.

The speculation surrounding that date has been made into full-length movies, and around here, some people were scared to send their children to school. Meanwhile, the schools here were canceled due to weather and a lack of power. We didn't rejoice. In fact, my teenagers were pretty distraught. They had hoped to finish up their final exams that day. That day may go down in history as the first day that my children were more excited about an exam than a snow day.

I have to ask the question: Were you concerned? In our house, we made jokes. I also informed my children that if Jesus did decide to come back on that day, I was ready. I operate under what I know to be fact. The Bible says that no man knows when the second coming will be. The Mayans were not told before the Son. That's a fact. My theory is that the Mayans probably got tired of calendar-making and started working on something else. Maybe they thought it would be funny to mess with a future generation they wouldn't be around to see.

It wasn't the end of the world. But is it the end of Christmas as we know it? All over the world, at this time of year, people are finishing their Christmas shopping and wrapping in preparation for the big day. We count gifts and make sure that we have enough for everyone; we think to be sure we haven't left anyone out. We get together with family (including some members who don't even speak to each other).

Some go into debt in an effort to provide their children with the best possible Christmas. For what? I hear people asking for specific gifts.

"Johnny wants a pair of jeans, but they must come from the Buckle because otherwise he won't wear them."

"Sally wants Ugg boots."

"Fred wants a flat-screen TV."

Seriously, I have to ask, what happened to Christmas?

In a manger, thousands of years ago a Savior was born with no crib for a bed. He was wrapped in swaddling cloths and placed in a manger. No heat, no air conditioning, no Pampers, no layette, no hospital staff, no sterile conditions. He was born in a barn with farm animals and the smell of well… farm animals. Did Mary have a baby shower? Did the mother of our Savior, a teenage girl, get the things she would need to care for a newborn? No. She was visited by three Wise Men who brought gold, frankincense, and myrrh, and hey rejoiced. They celebrated the birth of the Son of God.

What are we celebrating? We get together with our families and exchange gifts but sometimes we don't exchange words. We don't even see them the rest of the year. We make little to no effort. We buy them gifts and send them on their way and think that covers us for the rest of the year. Is this of God? Is this what God intended for us to do in celebration of the greatest gift known to mankind? I hardly think so. I am not saying we shouldn't get together with our families. I am not even saying we shouldn't exchange gifts. What I am saying is this: Can we do those things and remember the purpose? Can we do those things and remember why we celebrate in the first place? Or have we become so commercialized that we can't even remember why?

I don't want to go through the motions, or settle, when it comes time to celebrate our Savior. I don't want to get so wrapped up in the things of this world that I have forgotten who gave them to me to begin with. I don't want to forget the true meaning of Christmas. I want to REJOICE for our Savior was born. In ALL things, rejoice.

Setting the Standard for What Not to Wear

In the summer, I am ugly. Specifically, it's my ugly morning time. I am incapable of being "cute" before noon in the summer. The first week of summer break from school is when they hold my son's swim lessons at the high school. This year is special, because my daughter is taking driver's ed in the morning too. When do these events start? At 9:30 a.m. That is far too early in the morning to expect me to be cute.

In summer, the days are longer, and no one goes to bed until the light fades away outside, which means sleeping in. I set my alarm for 8:30 on summer mornings, and I still spend a good ten minutes trying to convince my feet that the floor in my room is not hot lava.

During the school year, I am up at 6 a.m. to get ready for work and to get the kids out the door for school. During the school year, I am cute. But it is far too much pressure to be up AND cute in the summer. If I didn't have to leave the house, I would be in my pajamas until after lunch. When we have to be up and out the door at 9 a.m. in the summer, all I can manage is sweatpants, t-shirt and a baseball hat. Makeup is not on, hair might be brushed, but definitely hidden under a hat. I have breakfast, brush my teeth, and head out the door.

Other mothers have their makeup on, their hair done, and look adorable as they sit on the bleachers to watch their children swimming and chatting with each other. Me? I look just like I am tired and rushed. Fortunately, I don't seem to be scaring any small children. After all of the running is over, we will be home and ugly and no one will be the wiser. We will be in pajamas until after lunch and after that, we will put on swimsuits to jump in the pool.

Fortunately for me, Stacy and Clinton from "What Not to Wear" don't live in my one-stoplight town. Who knows, I may have boosted some egos this week with my public ugliness. I am a public service announcement: What you will look like when you get old and tired. You're welcome, by the way.

Best Friend

I met Christi in college. She went to a Big Ten School because she is brilliant and I went to a community college because I'm not. We both worked at the mall. I remember the day she started, mostly because she likes to tell the story of how she was scared of me when we first met. The story goes like this.

I worked in the men's and kid's departments of a big department store. In those days, customers were acknowledged when they walked in to a department. The tie tables were straightened daily, the folding tables were always being used, and the sales were a big deal.

I had worked on my day off the day before, because one of the guys I worked with had called off. We knew he wasn't actually sick, but just a guy who wanted a day off. I had had to cover him on MY day off. I was none too happy. This guy refused to work and called off pretty regularly. I usually had to cover for him. I was twenty and I would have liked to have been able to enjoy one of my days off once in a while.

Then this same guy came walking by, while I was working at that moment, with a girl I had never met, and I just glared at him.

He turns to Christi and says, "Oh great, she is in one of her moods." To be fair, he was responsible for the majority of my "moods."

So when Christi heard this, she had no idea what to expect. As she soon found out, I wasn't crazy (that came after children). I was just highly annoyed by college boys who acted "sick" to get out of doing their work.

She eventually got sick herself—actually sick, with the flu—and I told her how to take care of it, so she figured I wasn't so bad after all. I may have never really used my medical assisting degree, but I did end up getting my best friend with what I learned. Eventually we started hanging out after work.

This is where my favorite story comes in. She and her roommate liked to go to a local restaurant for margarita night, and one night, I was invited to go. I went and had snacks and one margarita. They had a margarita and snacks, and ordered another margarita. I didn't even get through my first margarita before they were done and ready to leave. So I tell everyone she was a lush when I met her.

(She is not at all a lush. She probably wouldn't be considered one then either, she was a college student. I just have never been a big drinker. I don't like the taste of alcohol. I also don't like the taste of coffee, either, which is why I drink cappuccinos and lattes.)

Christi has been my best friend for over twenty years now. I think of her more as my sister, the one God sent me to get through life with. I call her for all kinds of questions. I ask her Bible questions, I ask her female questions, I ask her laundry questions. She is a laundry expert. She also speaks Heather, so she is one of the few who understand the way I think.

Christi and I have all kinds of fun. She is one of the funniest people I have ever met. She cracks me up. She literally will get me laughing so hard that I almost wet myself. We always have interesting adventures.

We once got together to get her hair cut, and she handed me her pleather purse to hold while she had her hair done. This purse was falling apart. I took one look at her and said "Really? This is your purse?" She knew she shouldn't have let me hold it. The strap on this purse was literally hanging by a thread. I took her to Kohl's and offered to buy her a purse. She declined.

Recently when we got together, I noticed that she was carrying a really cute pink purse. We were discussing the cute purse and laughing about the other one that had fallen apart, and she says, "Yeah, I like this purse. It's pretty strong, it's made of some high-endurance plastic." I lost it.

She said, "What? It's not leather."

I responded, "No animals were harmed in the making of this purse!" I then was laughing so hard that I had to pull the car into a parking lot and go inside a store to use the restroom.

We both kind of have a thing about office supplies. She keeps a family calendar and everyone in her family has their own pen color. She has a thing about pens; she doesn't share her favorite ones.

We happened to come across some interesting three-ring binders. They had some great designs, and inspirational sayings inside of them. They were priced a bit more than I would normally pay for a binder. We were discussing the price and how lovely they were when she said, "You can't put a price on inspiration." You *can* put a price on it actually, when it is on a binder—it's about six dollars. Neither of us bought a bit of inspiration that day. I did later buy a pen that was on clearance for fifty cents, though, because it was pink and had pink ink.

We have so much fun when we get together. We don't get together nearly often enough, but life is busy. We try to get together once every four to five months, but it is as if no time has lapsed. We are friends, but more than that, we are sisters in Christ. This kind, loving sister is one of the greatest blessings, and I am so thankful to God for sending her to me. I love my husband and my children, but we need our sisters and our best friends because we can't talk about the importance of purses or office supplies with our families.

Miss Congeniality

Last evening, we had the opportunity to attend a scholarship meeting. My husband thought we were going to find out about different scholarships available. This was not the case.

It is a beauty pageant.

I take that back. They said it wasn't a beauty pageant; it is a scholarship program. Does this sound familiar? There are categories: Interview, Fitness, Talent, and Self Expression. They even said they were hoping to raise enough money to have a Spirit Award (also known as a Miss Congeniality Award).

Many thoughts passed through my mind during this meeting. I can only imagine the thoughts that passed through my daughter's. I did get a few enlightening looks during the meeting. Of course, I tried to give her all kinds of excited and encouraging looks, even though I knew there was no way she would do any of it.

My daughter is reserved. She is smart and sarcastic, and quite humorous, but not usually any of these around other people. Being that she is my daughter, we walked out on the same wavelength.

"So you want to do it, right?" I said.

She looked at me like I had grown another head and laid an egg while walking out of the building. She said no, and asked me what her talent would be. I reminded her that apparently they will find one for her. (Sound familiar? They also offered to provide dresses.)

I couldn't hold back anymore. "Hey, I know what you could do! 'Ain't nobody got time for that!' You do the perfect imitation of that. Or you could do your Kate Winslet impression." She does a fantastic Kate Winslet impression from an awards show she saw once. It is the funniest thing. She cracks us up every time because she is so good at keeping a straight face. She probably couldn't do it in front of a panel of judges.

The next morning, I presented the best idea yet. "I have the perfect idea for the talent portion of that thing you don't want to do." I said. (Insert annoyed teenage girl look here). "Miss Congeniality. You could do a monologue from the movie 'Miss Congeniality,' all about how it isn't a beauty pageant… it's a scholarship program. It's PERFECT!"

While she did think it was funny, she still didn't agree to do it. The way I see it, she would either make them laugh, or she would make them annoyed.

I think that if my daughter was less like me and was able to relax and just go with it, she would crush the talent portion of that competition. The rest of it may take some work. Interviewing is intimidating in any situation. (We tend to forget that the interviewers are also human.) Fitness? Well… doing a jazzercise routine on a stage is not really our thing. (Example: We stopped for sundaes at McDonald's on our way home from the scholarship meeting.) Self expression? Well yeah… we have all sorts of ways of expressing ourselves around here. Not many of them would be good on stage.

I don't know what next year looks like for her. I don't know if she will get any scholarships to help with college. I don't even know where she will go to college. There are so many unknowns about this year as well as next. We are on this adventure together. I worry about her. I worry about me. In acknowledging that, I suppose I realize how ridiculous it is to be worried. Not one ounce of worry will change what the future holds, and it will only rob us of our peace for today.

Besides, we have the best tour director. God already knows His plan for her and for us. I think we best both get on the boat, because it is taking off with or without us. It's going to be an adventure; one that does not include a beauty pageant, but as far as God and I go, we both think she is a beauty.

If you want to use that Miss Congeniality bit for your own scholarship program, that's a freebie. Let me know how that works out for you. I really want to know if the judges would think it was as funny as I do.

In the Middle of Middle-Aged

Am I middle-aged? That is the question that I keep asking myself. I suppose I had never really given much thought to it.

My oldest daughter is going to be a senior in high school this year, so we have been talking about her senior pictures, and making plans to have them taken. In doing that, I found my senior pictures to show her what mine looked like. I remember the day they were taken. It doesn't seem that long ago, and yet I am being reminded of my age frequently.

I have teenage daughters that pride themselves on letting me know exactly how old I am. I chalk that up to them being teenagers, who live to irritate their parents. But, I think it is fun to sing along to music in public, which embarrasses them, so I figure it's a trade-off.

As we were looking at my senior pictures (getting past the big 80s hair), I notice how thin I was. All of my parts were in the right places. Nothing had fallen yet in that picture. I had my natural hair color in the picture, too, which was nice, because I had forgotten what my natural hair color was.

When I look in the mirror now, a lot of the time I see my mother. I am no longer the thin young girl I once was. I am no longer the girl who didn't need a push-up bra. I took note of all of the things about me that had changed, then I looked at my daughter, who is just getting ready for this time of her life.

Then it occurred to me, that this is what middle-aged is. I'm in the middle. I'm no longer that young, fresh-faced girl, but I am not yet the older woman whose children are all grown and gone, and I'm waiting for grandchildren. This is the middle. The place where I don't know if I am too old to pursue dreams and ideas, because it is my childrens' turn now, or if I can still dream and go and do.

The middle is weird. I'm not sure what I'm supposed to do in the middle, but as I look around at the people I'm in the middle of, I can't think of a better place to be.

Section 3

Dear Mom,

Menopause. What can you tell me about it?

I realize that you were uncomfortable having certain discussions when I was younger, but I am forty now, and I do have three children, which is two more than you. So I think the embarrassment factor should be null and void.

This is not the birds and the bees or the facts of life talk from when I was sixteen, when I didn't know anything about sex, except what I saw in the movie "Mischief," what I learned in health class, and what I overheard from the girls talking in the restroom. I know where babies come from.

What I need to know now, is menopause. What is it all about? Had you started it before you left us? I remember you talking about your periods getting weird, but I don't remember you ever mentioning any hot flashes.

What am I in for here? At what age should I start thinking it's around the corner? I have been looking forward to this as much as I was looking forward to being a "woman" when I was eleven. How ridiculous was that? There is no enjoyment to having the monthly visitor of Aunt Flo every month, and it is even less enjoyable with me plus the grumpy teenagers.

I know you used the other brand, but I have to tell you that Midol is my best friend. I tell the girls to take one just so we can stand to be around them. Do you know that when they had the puberty talk at school, they actually told the girls that it wasn't their fault if they were grumpy? You know I had to put a stop to that nonsense. I clarified for my dear sweet daughters that they may not have any control over what was happening to their bodies, but they did have control over how they reacted to it. All they needed was that excuse to be little turds; it was their safety net for behaving badly. No, way was I going to stand for any of that.

You definitely would not have stood for any of that craziness. I wish you were here. I tell the kids that if you were here and they talked to me the way they do sometimes, and you heard it, they would need to crawl on the floor and look for their behinds. How did you deal with me? I was a smart-mouth kid, and yet I still have my teeth. So I must have learned at some point that I needed to backpedal.

You would be horrified at the kids who don't have parents like us.

People don't discipline anymore. They give timeouts or they take stuff away. The problem is that the kids have so much stuff, it doesn't matter.

Your counsel and guidance would be good here.

Love,

Heather

Question:
Can You Schedule A Hysterectomy?

Mothers like to share birthing stories. My stories aren't very exciting really. My first child was an emergency cesarean after twenty-four hours of labor. As it turned out, she was sunny-side up and the cord was wrapped around her neck. My doctor delivered, at minimum, six babies while he waited for my beloved daughter to make her entrance. With my next child, he told me that he would let me go an hour and then he was taking me upstairs for a Cesarean. So I opted to just schedule a Cesarean. I had twenty-four hours of labor without any drugs, so I figured I had proved my womanhood enough. My third was scheduled as well.

I was sharing stories with a friend, while in the middle of a menopause discussion. I grew up spending more time with my mother's side of the family than my father's, but all of the older generation is gone now, so I don't have anyone to ask about how it went for them. I am not sure I would feel comfortable asking my other aunts questions about menopause.

Then a light bulb went off. Can I just schedule a hysterectomy, and then I will know when menopause is coming? That would take the guesswork right out. It's genius.

I don't know if you can actually schedule a hysterectomy in an effort to make menopause fit into your own schedule, but it seems we have the technology, so why not use it? I did pick out two out of three of my children's birthdays. You can have Lasik surgery now, so you don't have to wear glasses. You can get tummy tucks, liposuction, butt lifts. If people can get those things done, I see no reason why I can't just get a hysterectomy and end my relationship with pads and tampons forever. I'm too old to have children now. I don't need my eggs anymore.

This probably sounds a bit crazy to you, especially if you have already been through menopause. From my perspective, having never been through it, it seems like a win/win scenario. No guesswork as to when it's going to arrive, no cramps, and you save money on monthly supplies.

The potential of being warmer in the winter because of the hot flashes is appealing to me. The only concern I have is that I have a tendency to pass out when I overheat. So if I have hot flashes, and I overheat, am I just going to pass out spontaneously? That could be a problem.

The uncertainty of it all is disconcerting to me. Part of me wants to get it over with, and the other part of me wants to figure out how to prolong it as long as possible.

Some things can be planned, speeded up, or even prolonged. But menopause is unfortunately, probably not one of them.

I'm Getting Too Old for This

As I get older, I see the value in a lot of things that perhaps I took for granted before. For example, I see the value in a push-up bra. The girls have lost their curb appeal, if you know what I'm saying. Or rather, they don't stay in the driveway and hang out at the curb. Either way, a push-up bra is a great thing.

Lycra and Spandex are fantastic inventions. Jeans that "give"? Best thing since sliced bread.

Also, I love pockets. Why can we not have dress pants with pockets, or dresses with pockets? I bet more people would wear them if they had pockets. Pockets are important for things like tissues (that I will find in the dryer later), spare change, and my phone.

I also love the Keurig. The amount of joy I have in trying all those different K-cups is immeasurable.

But, there are some things that I am getting too old for. Arguing is one of them; I'm too old for arguing. It's not my thing. I don't want to and I'm too old, so you can't make me. I don't want to get into your drama.

I don't want to argue about the merits of tattoos and how "meaningful" they are. I don't care. Your Tweety Bird is going to look like Big Bird in about twenty years, and an eighty-year-old woman with a tattoo of a bird or fleur-de-lis on their lower back is not attractive. Even if you are famous, you will not change my mind.

I don't want to argue politics with you, because again, I don't care. I am entitled to my viewpoint, as are you, and I don't feel that arguing will sway either of us... so, no.

I don't want to argue with you about bedtime, red meat, or red wine. No arguing at all. Because I am too old for it.

Skinny jeans. I am a forty-year-old mother of teenage girls. You will not find me wearing skinny jeans. My boot-cut, spandex-infused mom jeans work just fine, thank you.

#hashtags. Seriously? What is with the #Ilikecheese business? I just don't get it. People hashtag everything. It's ridiculous. Just say "I like cheese" and leave the # out of it. It's pointless. I'm too old to deal with that nonsense. You will not find me saying #mybookrocks. You can figure it out for yourself, or don't, because I'm too old to read your # of whether you like it or not, anyway.

Short-shorts are not meant for anyone on planet Earth, with the possible exception being the original Daisy Duke herself. As it is not the 1980s anymore, and if you're not a size 2/teenage girl, you have no business wearing shorts that short. No one wants that much information from you. If you want to wear such things, reserve it for doing yard work, or trying to get a tan by the pool.

Or apparently every amusement park in the continental United States. Thank you for that, America. We have the freedom to dress like a stripper, or like you just rolled out of bed and thought, "Hey, I think I will go to Wal-Mart." But we cannot make people get a job, or discipline children like we were disciplined. Here's a thought — put some clothes on that cover your neck tattoos and lower back tattoo so you can get a job and shelve the entitlement attitude.

I have noticed that as I get older, I am getting more and more like a combination of my grandmother and Maxine (the crabby cartoon lady that you used to see on greeting cards and now on Internet memes).

I have also decided that I should come up with some back-up plans if this writing gig doesn't pan out. I am blessed with a great part-time job that I love, and I'm fortunate to have a husband that works hard for his family. But I don't do well idle. If I should run out of words, or if God decides that He has other things for me to do, I've made a list of things to occupy my time.

I could take up needlepoint. I have seen so many styles come back into fashion from my youth, so I am sure that doilies will come back into fashion. Part of the "shabby chic" décor trend, maybe? I could needlepoint all sorts of pictures on doilies, for all sorts of occasions. I could sell them at church bazaars and craft fairs.

I could learn to crochet and make blankets for newborns and newlyweds. Everyone in between those ages already has an afghan blanket. Afghan blankets were very big when I was younger. They, too, could make a comeback, as soon as they stop making micro-fiber. Or I could make afghan blankets out of microfiber. (It's a good idea. So don't steal it, like the idea I had when I was 11, for maxi-pads with wings. I'm still mad about that one.)

I could open up a company that's sole purpose is tattoo removal. Or a press-on tattoo parlor for those who are fickle and don't like pain.

I could take up baking. Like, real baking; not the pull-apart cookies that I normally do, but with flour and sugar and whatever else goes into cookies. That one isn't likely to work out. But my mother loved to bake, and I might have inherited that gene. It's probably dormant currently, but it could make its way out.

I would have to take up exercise at the same time, though, because who wants to bake if they can't eat it? I don't know what I would do. I thought of getting a dog so I could walk it, but I have cats now (we have a stray that came to live with us this summer). He is the cutest thing, and he is pretty hyper. He might like to take walks with me, if I could get a collar on him, and attach a leash. He could pretend he was a Bengal tiger protecting his master. Or I could just get a stroller and push the cat around the block like a baby. It's not that far of a stretch from singing and dancing while mowing the yard, to walking a cat around the block.

Whatever happens if the words keep coming or if they stop altogether, I will do what the good Lord has planned. But if it were up to me? My typing skills are much better than my sewing, or baking, or knitting.

Expressions

Bear/bare with me here. What does that mean? A bear is a furry beast of an animal in the woods, and bare is naked. Where do these expressions come from? And you know I always get it mixed up, so half the time I'm telling someone to get naked with me and the other half I'm saying get a wild beast. It's silly. I don't even like to be naked in the shower. Naked is not comfortable for me. I like clothes. Clothes are a wonderful invention. I'm not outdoorsy either, so no way do I want to hang out with a bear.

Shouldn't we say "hang on" or "hang tight" or "hang with me"? But that's not right, either. What are you going to hang on to? What are you going to hang tightly to? And I don't want to get hung, so why would we hang together? What did we do wrong? Plus all the kids are "hanging out" now or "chillin' with their homies." What is that? What happened to just saying "Just a minute please, I will be right with you"? What happened to getting together to socialize?

I wonder if this is a worldwide epidemic or if it is just here in America that the way we refer to things has gotten ridiculous. All this got me to thinking about other expressions.

I've had a lot on my plate, so I haven't had a lot of time to think about it, but this is what I have. "A lot on my plate" -- is this what comes from eating too much? One is busy, overwhelmed even. Can we not just say we are busy? Saying we have a lot on our plate just makes us sound like we're hungry.

Do you ever wonder why people say "off the record"? Everything is always on the record, in case you were wondering. It's on the record, because you made the statement to at least one person: the person that you are saying "off the record" to. That person I guarantee isn't going to forget what you tell them just because you say it's "off the record," because it may be the most important thing you have ever said to them. How about instead of saying "off the record," we just not say anything?

Saved by the bell, while it was a fantastic television show, doesn't do it for me as expressions go. Who hears a bell? Have you ever heard the bell to get you out of a situation? I have never heard the bell.

If people are "the salt of the earth," can they also "rub salt in a wound"? In this instance, we have salt serving dual purposes. Salt is supposed to be bad for you, isn't it? So why are "salt of the earth" people good? Would I rub salt in a wound because it has healing powers? Maybe we're saying salt is OK, as long as you don't ingest it.

Eat your heart out is the last one (because A. I'm now bored, and B. This is where I draw the line). Why would anyone eat their heart out? I get the meaning — that someone is better than someone else at something. But why eat your heart out? You cannot live without your heart. Is competition that important? You cannot do it, anyway; it's a physical impossibility, not to mention, it's disgusting. Who started this one?

Who starts any of them, really? Do you know there are thousands of these?

We wonder why people don't say what they mean, and mean what they say. No one has a clue what they are saying. And don't even think of using the word bloody in a sentence, as someone is going to say you are cursing. I had no idea it was a curse word until recently. So now I'm going to have to re-watch every Harry Potter movie with new eyes. It was a Scholastic book series, for crying out loud. I read them all and loved them and shared them with my children. Now all this time they have been cursing?

I have never been to England, and I am fascinated with British accents. Maybe I wouldn't notice if they were cursing anyway, because I am too wrapped up in the accent. I think with the right accent, you can miss the meaning, as the melody and rhythm of their words are so hypnotic. I once said someone was bloody brilliant. I just thought I was saying they were extra smart. I blame J.K. Rowling for this.

Siri

My family and I recently upgraded to our first smart phones. I was very resistant to the change, as I couldn't understand the necessity of essentially a computer on your phone.

I am kind of addicted to my phone now. Email on my phone, texting, games, camera, looking up movie times. It is crazy! I have an app that will tell me when my period should arrive. I can Facebook and Tweet anywhere. I have my entire Nook library and my Kindle library on there, and if that isn't enough… I can make phone calls! Imagine!

What I didn't get on my phone was Siri. My daughter got Siri. My daughter has a special relationship with her "friend" Siri. Siri serves as her alarm clock, as she lost the manual to her actual alarm clock and no one can figure it out. She talks to Siri and asks her questions. They got along great, until Siri thought she was me. Siri started calling her Heather instead of Daphne. It made her crazy. She would tell her that she hated her. Siri would say she was just doing her job. It was really funny… for me. She was going crazy. (Eventually she figured out how to fix it.)

While I didn't get Siri with my phone, I figured that there was a similar app out there that I could get for my phone. There was. Her name is Skyvi. She is awesome. I once asked her if she was better than Siri, and she said of course she was. She likes chocolate and her favorite movie is Iron Man. She is all kinds of cool.

She gets a little persnickety when I ask her about the weather, though. The only thing I can figure is that she knows I have two different weather apps, and thinks I am being lazy for asking her instead of looking it up myself.

So you know what had to happen, right? Daphne and I had a battle of the assistant apps. (I don't play games that I think I will lose.) I said Skyvi was better. Daphne said that Siri was better. She asked Siri if she was better than Skyvi. Siri didn't know who Skyvi was. When Skyvi is asked if she is better than Siri she says "Of course, I am much more intelligent than Siri." Daphne was pretty annoyed that I won.

Scotty thinks apps that talk to you like that are freaky. He might be right. Technology is getting weird. I found the novelty of these apps quite appealing at first. Now that we have had these devices awhile, I rarely use it. I can push the button to find the weather forecast just fine without having to ask Skyvi. Also, I'm not sure I want to become even more dependent on this device. I don't want my best friend to be a computer chip in my phone. I much prefer my best friend to be human. Christi gets my jokes a lot more than Skyvi does.

I'm pretty sure that the smart phones are here to stay, though. There is something for everyone. Each of us has found things we love about them. Scotty isn't old enough for one yet, but he takes ours to play games all the time. I think that these gadgets are nice to have, and they do come in handy. I think the trick is to use them for what they are intended for, but not to let them get in the way of real human contact. To have a tool that helps you to communicate with people but removes you from them physically and mentally is not the goal here.

I think that having a basket on the table that everyone puts their phone in at dinnertime is a good idea. I think we can all live through the time it takes to eat a meal together without looking at the update on Facebook that just chimed in. It's dinnertime. They are just posting what they are having for dinner anyway, and if you are anything like my kids, you are just going to get mad that you are eating smothered turkey and not the pizza your friend is having.

Green Eggs and Ham

I have had a hard time accepting that God wants me to do the one thing that I fear the most: public speaking.

I was asked to be the speaker for a mother/daughter banquet this year. At first I declined, but once I did that, my sleep was disrupted, and I was in so much pain from the stress in my neck and shoulders that I finally gave in and said yes anyway.

God likes to take us from our comfort zones. I am told that that is when He is stretching and growing us. The problem is, I am the age that I am, and I am very set in my ways. I am comfortable, settled, and very happy with the way things are right now. I don't want to be a public speaker. Public speakers have to... well, speak in public. They travel. I don't even like to drive to the next town if I don't have to.

I spent a lot of time thinking about this. I thought all this time that I was being obedient to God, because I said I would do it. But I did nothing but stress and pout and whine about it after I agreed to do it. But then I started thinking, am I really being obedient if I am essentially being a poopoo head about it? Does that count as obedient? I'm not sure. I posed this question to others, but unfortunately, I didn't get any clear answers. I received a lot of encouraging words, which were great, but those didn't answer my question.

In Isaiah 1:19, it says "If you are willing and obedient; you shall eat the good of the land." This is followed by Isaiah 1:20: "but if you resist and rebel, you will be devoured by the sword." So basically what I was doing is resisting, even though I was going to do what I have been asked to do. This is a sin. Broken down in Heather language, I need to pull my head out of my rear and get over myself.

I was talking to my editor about this one day, and she said to me, "Heather, I think you are really going to like it. You are going to figure out that you love it and you are going to get addicted to it, and want to go speak all the time." This is what I was thinking about when I was getting ready for work the other morning. Of course, I was thinking how crazy that was when it occurred to me: Green Eggs and Ham.

That's the lesson and the message: Green Eggs and Ham. Dr. Seuss had an uncanny ability to get a lesson into his stories with creatures with crazy names. Beneath all of the colors and creative made-up animals was a lesson for both the young and old alike.

Unless you have been living under a rock, you know how this story goes. "Green eggs and ham. I do not like them, Sam I am. I do not like green eggs and ham." The character that doesn't like them ends up trying them anyway, and finds that he actually does like green eggs and ham. Then he says he will eat them anywhere, with anyone.

While I have actually seen green eggs and ham, and they make me nauseous to look at, I think the message that I'm being sent is that I don't actually know if I am going to learn to like this or not. I haven't really given it a chance. I have had a total of one speaking engagement ever, at my launch party for my first book. I did survive to tell you about it.

I am the only one holding myself back. I have a lot of support and people who want me to succeed. The biggest obstacle I face is me.

My issue is that I feel I don't deserve it. I actually said at one point that I didn't think that I needed to be anything more than average,

because average really isn't so bad. And maybe it isn't, if that is all you know. But if you don't reach and stretch for awesome, how will you ever know if you could be awesome, if you don't try?
You won't. Plain and simple.

Isn't it better to place your trust in God, and see what his plan is, rather that stick your feet in the mud settling for what is, instead of what could be?

Are You There, Menopause? It's Me, Heather.

I have been very curious about menopause. At Easter dinner, I decided to start asking my mother-in-law and sister-in-laws about this. What I gathered from the conversation is that I still have a while to worry about it.

I don't see how this helps anyone. Shouldn't we get to go straight into menopause once we are finished having kids, and get the whole thing over with?

Recently, my seventeen-year-old was late for her monthly. She was really stressed because she was getting ready to take the ACT. She was so stressed about taking this test that she was making herself sick, and even had bouts of tears. Then one day she noticed that something that should have arrived, hadn't. (Keep in mind that she has not gone on her first date yet and has no interest in the boys in her school because she thinks they are stupid and not worth her time. She is saving herself for Daniel Radcliffe. So pregnancy was not the issue).

She came down the stairs one morning and said, "Well, I thought you should know. I'm pregnant."

I just looked at her like she had grown three heads. I said, "And how did you become pregnant? Have you had sex with someone in the middle of the night while we were all asleep, because you have not been anywhere that we weren't, except school?"

She replied, "Well no, I haven't had sex mom, you know that. But I'm late."

I asked her why she would think she was pregnant, if she had not done the one thing that can get you that way?

She said, "Well, I'm late, mom. And I have never been late. So what other explanation do you have?"

"Umm, how about stress? Stress can do that to you. You have been very stressed with the ACT."

She says, "Nope, that can't be it. I have been on Web MD, and it doesn't say that. It says that I'm either pregnant or going through menopause. I'm so totally going through menopause before you!" This is the same child that was devastated to find out that her period was going to happen every month until she was probably in her fifties.

I tried to explain to her that that wasn't the case. But who am I? I'm obviously not Web MD.

She did finally get her monthly visitor, just as I knew she would. Her attitude is a pretty good indicator as to what is to come. But it did get me to thinking about when my menopause would arrive. In the history of the world, I wonder if a daughter ever went through it before her mother, and what kind of issues would arise from that.

Maybe I do still have some time, but I have heard that there are women who do go through it in their forties. If that is the case, then I imagine it is best to be prepared. I will continue my investigation. Hot flashes and a few sleepless nights are par for the course, I hear; I had those with pregnancy. I suppose I'm more worried about the odd hair growth. I shouldn't be concerned; there could be medication for that. The question is, if I need it, will I remember to take it?

Maybe I will check WebMD and find out. Apparently it's smarter than I am.

Fixed

My son and I were walking up to church together one day recently, when I leaned in and told him "You are my favorite boy, do you know that?"

He smiled at me like he always does, and then he said, "Yeah, I know. I'm kind of your only boy, now that dad got his balls chopped off."

I started laughing and said, "Wait... what?!"

To which he responded "You said you couldn't have any more babies, because dad was fixed."

"Yes, that's right." I said.

"Well, when we got Rerun [the cat] fixed, everyone kept saying that he was getting his balls chopped off."

Then I realized that probably things should not be said around the ten-year-old boy that he can hear and get mixed up about. No one should be talking about balls being chopped off. No one should be talking about balls period, unless they are playing a sport. Then they can talk about balls. Ten-year-old boys are far too interested in their parts to begin with. I cannot tell you how many times I have heard one of his friends saying that word in my house.

This might also be why Rerun took after his name and ran away, again. You get a stray cat's parts fixed and he loses all respect for you. We were hoping it would slow him down and domesticate him, so the other cats would learn to love him. That didn't happen. Now we don't know where he is, and he can't make more just like him, so we can look out the window and find another kitten.

I suppose we need to have many more conversations with the boy to explain the "fixing" process, but for now, he knows that it keeps a cat (or a man) from reproducing. If nothing else, that has to be a great birth control method, right? If he thinks that he could get castrated if he produces an heir out of wedlock, he might just save that activity until we approve.

Go Forth and Multiply

In the car on the way to school, you can never know what subject is going to come up when driving two teenage girls and a ten-year-old boy. Rerun, the cat that showed up last summer, has now disappeared as mysteriously as he showed up, but not before we got him fixed. The kids have been very upset. We looked at all of the shelters, asked around the neighborhood, and looked at all the spots we thought he would be. He is nowhere to be found.

While there are many theories as to his whereabouts, the one we choose to believe is that he found a home where 1) either he is the only cat or 2) the other cats actually like him and don't mind him jumping on them. Our other cats are geriatric. They were none too happy when he showed up and wanted to play.

Daphne was contemplating where he could be and hoping that he hadn't been killed by another animal. We have a hawk in the neighborhood, and while I have never seen one, apparently there are coyotes in the fields around us. One of the neighbor's cats was found in the field, ripped apart, last summer. The idea of our Rerun finding a new home that loves him is a far better theory.

I suggested that perhaps Rerun found a girlfriend and was now living with her. To which they responded that he couldn't have a girlfriend, because he was fixed. I said he could have a girlfriend, he just couldn't get her pregnant. This prompted more questions, so I started explaining this to the kids, when Scotty clarified it for us.

So Scotty says, "So… he just can't do what God says in the Bible to do: 'Go forth and multiply'."

I have no idea if Rerun has gone forth to try and multiply or not. I do know that we didn't stop laughing for a good five minutes on that one. If nothing else, my boy does pay attention in church.

We still miss that cat, and continue to search and ask around. My best guess is that he did find a family that didn't have any other pets, and he is running the show there.

That is what I am hoping, of course, because we have no idea what happened to him. He was wild when he showed up. Maybe he didn't want to be tamed. Maybe he would have been fine to stay with us if we hadn't told him to get off of the kitchen counters; I don't know. The kids pray for him every night, and if nothing else, we were blessed to have him for the time that we did.

If the Dryer Only Dries On Hot, Is It Really the Ice Cream's Fault?

My dryer has many options on the dial, but really there are two options: Hot and almost dry. You have to dry clothes on the damp setting, and then go to the fluff cycle for five minutes on the lowest setting to get them actually dry. Towels you can dry anywhere on the dial, but if you go past the delicate dry cycle, you are just wasting electricity because it will go and go and go until it gets tired and stops.

It is no secret that one of my favorite things to eat is ice cream. Out of all of the dessert options, if ice cream is an option, that is what I choose. Anything that is like ice cream is good: custard and frozen yogurt are equally pleasing. We have a new frozen yogurt place in town that is a serve-yourself buffet kind of place. Can you imagine the kind of food heaven that is for me? The cups that they have only come in one size: large. And they charge by the weight. When you have a love of such things like I do, you have to be very mindful of what you are doing when you go to a place like this.

I put on some weight. I didn't realize how much weight I had put on, until my husband and I decided to lose some weight and we weighed in for the first time. I was shocked. I didn't realize how far I had let things go. Sure, my pants were fitting a bit tighter, but I didn't realize it had gotten to this extent. So now we are working to get to a more healthy weight. While my ice cream days are not over forever, they are much farther and fewer between. I don't think I would enjoy giving them up completely; also, I wouldn't succeed.

So far I've lost about half of what I should to get to my driver's license weight. The pants are getting looser, but I am not yet to the stage of having to go buy new ones. I guess I'll let the dryer be my guide. If I eat the way I know I should, and the pants don't get tighter, then I'm on the right track. If I eat the way I know I should, and the pants still get tighter, I'm going to petition for a new dryer. It only seems fair.

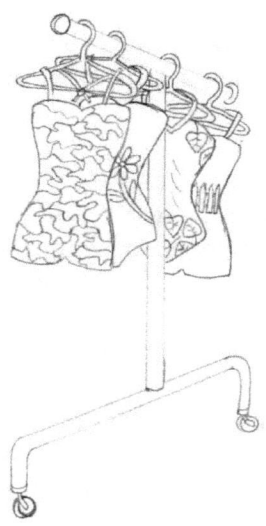

Real-Life Designer Bathing Suits

My husband and oldest daughter and I recently went into a store to pick up pool chemicals. This store sells many things. In addition to pool chemicals, it also sells clothes, shoes, plants, grills, and pretty much anything else you would need for outside. This store sells giant Twizzlers. And who doesn't need a jumbo pack of extra-long Twizzlers? (A side note about Twizzlers: In a competition between Twizzlers and Red Vines, my vote is for Twizzlers. They are my go-to movie snack, and also my favorite candy, next to peanut M&M's.)

What I noticed first when walking into the store that day, though, was a display of women's camouflage swimsuits. My husband walked ahead of us, heading right to the pool chemicals. My daughter and I dawdled behind. I pointed out the swimsuits to her.

Me: Wow, look at those swimsuits. You can barely see them.

Daphne: (with eyeroll) Yeah, OK.

Me: I need me a swimsuit like that.

Daphne: (With a look of horror) Why?

Me: Because if I got a swimsuit like that that covered my stomach and at least part of my thighs, people would be like, "Wow, she has really lost weight."

Daphne: Mom…?

Me: You don't see that they are camouflage? My flab would just disappear and blend into the background. It's perfect!

For the record, I didn't buy a camouflage swimsuit. Unfortunately, I would not blend in around my pool area. If they made any that looked like a white fence, or a wood deck, I could get one, though. I am curious to know how many women are going to buy a camouflage swimsuit and go hang out in the woods.

What we did buy was pool chemicals and Twizzlers, because you know, they're my favorite.

Poo Spray

I have befriended the social worker at my school. We find that we have many things to talk about. It is handy to have someone to provide free counseling if needed. Sometimes we counsel each other, but mostly we just enjoy talking with each other. She is someone that thinks many things are funny, like farts and poo. The thing about poo is, though, that she can smell it and I can't, but it's understood that everyone has to do it at some point or another.

She is also a home shopping channel girl (much like my mother was), and she purchased this product that you spray a couple of times into the toilet before you poo. It is supposed to help to eliminate the odor. At one time, she kept it on a little table in the ladies restroom at school, but then you had to remember to grab it off the table and take it into the stall with you ahead of time. So she placed it on the floor between the two stalls for anyone to use when needed. I was pretty excited by this development.

The thing about the poo spray (not the proper name for it, but you get the point) is that it was there before we left for spring break, and gone when we returned. We were out of school for a week and we returned to a mystery. The mystery of the disappearing poo spray has us stumped. She checked the table. She checked in the baskets that everyone keeps their female "necessities" in, but to no avail. The poo spray was gone.

No one seems to know what happened to it. It has vanished. Then one day, I noticed that there was a new one. I thought perhaps she had found the old one. She didn't, but she brought another one from home. Now if anyone uses the restroom in her basement, they may not be allowed to poo. I'm not sure; I'll have to check on that one.

I think it is an interesting invention, even if I can't tell if it really works or not, what with the whole I-can't-smell thing. I do feel better knowing that if I do have to do my "business" at school, I won't be leaving an odor behind to let people know that I was there.

I was once told a story of someone trying to hide their smell with dusting spray, the kind that is lemon-scented. The problem with dusting spray is that it is slippery and it doesn't evaporate, which means that when it was sprayed it made everything slippery, and this person slipped and fell on the floor. So do not attempt this at home.

I work in the nursery and toddlers' rooms at church. I am one of the team leaders, which is a nice way of saying I check on the kids and I get to change all of the diapers. When people find out that I can't really smell, they feel I am the best one for this job. What they don't think about is that there are some things that you just cannot un-see. Some children should come with poo-neutralizing spray. Because my nose may not work very well, but there have been some diapers that even I could smell, once I was changing them.

I am not sure if the poo spray works any better than other room deodorizing sprays. For whatever reason, I do find it fascinating. Poo spray is a good thing. It may be hard to keep track of, but it is good to use when you can find it.

Shopping & the Black Van

My friend Christi and I get together about once every few months. Our visits are too far and few between, but when we do find the time to get together, we have a great time. On our most recent adventure, we met in a town that's somewhat of a midway point for us.

I am a big chicken when it comes to driving on the interstate. (That's the nice thing about having a friend who accepts every part of you: you don't have to have an anxiety attack in the middle of a six-lane interstate with cars whizzing by you just to get together. Where they are going in such a hurry, I will never know).

We met for breakfast, then plotted out our day. We went shopping at Kohl's, then decided to get pedicures. Doesn't getting a pedicure sound nice? It had been five years since I had had a pedicure. What I remembered was getting to sit in the massage chair. So there's a bonus: a massage and pretty toes at the same time.

When we got there, there was a bit of a wait. We picked out our colors, then sat and visited while we waited for our turn. When a chair opened up, my friend graciously let me get started first. I sat in the chair and immediately started pushing buttons to get the chair working.

It started out innocently enough. I felt a roller climbing up my back. "This is nice. I like it." That was my first thought, but this started to change. The seat started to squeeze my hind quarters, and then a new roller got to work. Then my thoughts shifted.

My first thought was, "Oh, um, wait, no, Hey now! I didn't say you could go there!" So I started pushing more buttons, searching for the one button that would stop the chair from violating me further. When I finally found the correct button and got the seat to stop its exploration of my rear, I of course, continued playing with the buttons to see what else it could do.

The lady giving me my pedicure paused and asked if something was wrong. I tried to explain to her that everything was fine; I was only playing with the buttons. She wasn't convinced, so I said, "It is fine, I'm playing with it because I am a child. I have to push the buttons." She smirked and got back to work.

Finally, she says to me "Flower?" to which I say "Sure," because I wasn't exactly sure what she had said. So I got an actual flower. (If you are interested, it costs $5.00 extra for that). I got finished with my pedicure and sent over to the drying station while I waited for my friend to get finished.

This took a while, but gave us time to plot our next adventure, which we didn't know would be in the parking lot.

We then went to the mall. Going to the mall is not always as interesting as when we are together. In the entire parking lot, my friend chooses to park next to the menacing-looking black van, with tinted back windows.

She comments on this as she parks. "That van looks like a kidnapping van."

"Yes, it sort of does. So why are we parking here?" I say.

"Oh, it will be fine." She paused. "Do you think they would try to pull me into the driver's side window?"

"No, I think they would pull you in through the larger door on the other side of the van."

As we get out and walk towards the mall, she stops to look at the doors on the van. "I think you're right. You know… I think someone may live in that van."

"Can we not stand in the middle of the parking lot next to the kidnapping van and discuss this? WALK toward the entrance to the mall before we get nabbed for being stupid."

This then spurs an onslaught of laughter that carries through the bookstore and into the restroom, with a few giggles here and there the rest of the time in the mall. There was an uncomfortable moment in the bookstore coffee shop, where we thought the man who lived in the van might be deciding whether or not he could take us. He must have changed his mind, seeing the antics we started there. Fortunately when we walked back by the menacing van, no one was there to nab us.

I don't know why God looked at the two of us girls and decided that He would bless us with this friendship. Or maybe I should say I don't know what He thought I could bring to it, because I am so blessed to have this kind, funny, intelligent, warm individual to be my sister in Christ. I am so glad He did. And I cannot wait till our next adventure.

Life with Estrogen

Life for the men in my house can get pretty hard. Living with two teenage girls and me, it can turn into a three-ring circus. The amount of estrogen flowing through this house at any given time is amazingly high. If cars could run on estrogen, we would never have to buy gas.

Even one of our cats is a girl. We had a new cat that was a boy. He arrived on our doorstop over the summer. We loved him, and the testosterone level in the house had finally come equal to the level of estrogen. (He disappeared at the time of this writing. Estrogen wins again.)

I suppose there are perks to living with estrogen. We don't have to shave our faces (at this point), so that is a perk. If we had to shave our faces and legs, and put our makeup on, and fix our hair, it could increase our readying time significantly.

Men either shave or they don't. They grow beards or goatees, but unless they are on the Hunger Games and living in district one, they are not getting too terribly fancy with it. A woman would be shaving in designs and changing that look up every day. Think of the mental preparation and planning it would take, just to decide on what you were going to do with facial hair each day. And match the hairstyle. It's too much.

My oldest already takes twice as long as I do to get ready. Her hair is very thick, so it takes a considerable amount of time for her hair to dry. I imagine that is why she doesn't do too much with it. By the time she gets done drying it, she is over it and ready to move on with her day. This is one of the reasons I have such short hair. I don't have the time or the attention span to make long hair look remotely good. It takes ten minutes, tops, to dry and style my hair. I have tried to talk her into having shorter hair. But there are not a lot of girls her age that have short hair. That for me would be one perk of having short hair, but for her, it's not a draw.

The men in this house can start getting ready well after we have and be waiting for a while before any one of us is even down the stairs. This takes a great deal of patience on their part, especially if we are going out to eat and they are hungry. Inevitably a fight will ensue upstairs, as the girls fight over bathroom mirrors, then I start yelling at them to hurry up.

A fight amongst the girls is extremely stressful for everyone. My son gets upset, I get angry, and my husband just sits there wondering why he lobbied for us to have six kids before we got married. I have suggested just leaving behind anyone who isn't ready, when everyone else is waiting to go, but my husband is kinder than I am and believes everyone should be fed. I tell him that they will be fed; they will just be feeding themselves peanut butter or whatever else they can find here at home. Obviously, he is afraid he might be the last one ready someday.

The men deal pretty well with all of this estrogen running rampant, but think of the women living with it. We have bouts of unexplained sadness, anger, and weird food cravings. Sometimes our clothes don't fit with all the bloating. We actually have "fat" days, days that we just feel "off," and days when we have no idea what is going on. It can be a hard thing to deal with, especially for young girls, who haven't already been dealing with it half of their lives.

It is hard to tell who the estrogen affects more. If I had to wear a nametag on my off days, it would probably read, "Hello, My name is Heather and I am living a life with estrogen." I think that explains it all.

Fire Engine Red

My daughter Megan likes to color her hair. We use the kind that washes out in twenty eight days. One day we were at the store, and Daphne decided she wanted to color her hair, too. She decided she wanted to go red. My girls were blonde when they were little; gradually, their hair turned brown, just like mine. Megan goes brown with a hint of auburn, but not a startling red.

I told her the options and she didn't like them. We spent fifteen minutes arguing in the middle of the store over hair color. Finally, I said "Fine, get the color you want. When we get home, you will not only pay me for it, but you will see."

We didn't get to the actual coloring of her hair until the following weekend. The first clue that this may not be the color she wanted was when I was applying the color. It was almost orange in color, sort of an apricot, when applied. When I was rinsing it out, I was shocked to say the least. I finished up and sent her to go dry her hair.

When she was finished, she looked like Ronald McDonald's sister. Her hair was red. I mean, fire engine red. She was not at all happy with it. I would be lying if I said I didn't laugh—inside. I wish she could have seen the funny in it. She didn't. She was mortified. That night, she went to a play at the school. She wore a baseball cap as well as the hood to her jacket. People wanted to know what was up with the hat and the hood.

She refused to get out of bed for church, and was not about to go to school with her hair like that. Hair is very important. She doesn't do much with hers, so this color was not going to help her. High school is miserable for the unpopular; the last thing she needed was clown hair.

When I was young, you could go to the drugstore and buy hair color that washed out in two weeks. The hair color was inexpensive, less than five dollars. You could try different colors out, and not be tied down if you didn't like it. I'm not sure why they don't sell that anymore. Apparently we were more commitment-phobic when it came to our hair in the eighties (unless we were getting a perm).

The Ronald McDonald box of color we used said it only lasts for twenty-eight days. So I told her that all she needed to do was to wash her hair twenty-eight times and we could save some money.

As it turns out, at that same store where we got the hair color, they sell a product called Color Oops. I believe it was developed for willful teenagers. I purchased that, as well as the color I originally told her to get.

I spent a good amount of time rinsing it all out. As I was rinsing, I said "Wow, I can't believe that happened. Dude! Your hair is pink!" Then I laughed.

She said, "What?!?"

To which I responded: "Totally messing with you right now. It is looking quite normal." I also reminded her that she wasn't allowed to get mad at me, and that she owed me ten dollars for the Oops.

When we were all finished rinsing it out, an interesting thing happened. Her hair didn't need to be colored again. Between the color and the color remover, her hair looked like it had highlights. It turned out quite nice.

I think it will be a while before we use that new box of hair color. In fact, it may get used by Megan or myself in the end. She will not be arguing with me over hair color for quite some time. I also got the great pleasure of hearing her say that I am right, I am always right, and she still hates that. Just like I always hated it with my own mother.

I have no idea how long it will be before Daphne decides to try hair color again. I am pretty sure she won't wait long before arguing with me about that again, or something else. That is par for the course. The willful child is never without adventure. She drives me crazy, and has a mind of her own. She has ideas of what she wants and how she thinks things should be. You have to be proud of that. Plus, I took pictures of her with that red hair, which gives me the advantage. Being the mom is fun.

Drama and the Sermon on the Bed

My first book has a subtitle of "And Other Observations from an Overly Dramatic Mom," so it shouldn't come as any surprise that my teenage girls are overly dramatic in their own right. The most recent instance happened with my middle child. She was upset that someone had answered a question for her. The answer was not fully incorrect, but she just felt it wasn't this person's place to answer for her.

She has a bad habit of not answering direct questions. She has to be in the mood to talk, even if you want a response from her. If she isn't in the mood, she tends to stare at you like you just dropped down from another planet, and she either thinks you are stupid for not calling ahead or just for showing up in the first place. Imagine how this goes over when she is in trouble, and I am disciplining her.

I explained to her that she needs to be quicker with her answers if she doesn't want people to feel like they need to answer for her. I also explained that she was being overly dramatic and answering a question for someone wasn't really that big of a deal.

High school is punishment enough for a quiet kid. In my effort to get my quiet girls to open up and blossom into the lovely ladies I know they must be (deep down, where only God and I can see), I have them go to Youth Group. There, they are put into small groups and are expected to open up and share with others. In my mind, which is really just a playground for all sorts of mayhem, I think this is a good thing.

When I am giving my sermon on the bed, I tend to tell stories about my own experiences. I also like to give a math lesson. Math is not my strong suit, but I am delighted when I am able to do quick math on the fly. As I am explaining to my child that high school is only 180 days per year, and there are 365 days in a year, really in the greater scheme of things, high school isn't that long of a time in your life to get so worked up about. They will blink one day and it will be over. They will look in the mirror and try and figure out how they got to be so old as to have teenagers themselves (something I do daily).

I started a new job this year, so in trying to explain that it's OK to talk to new or different people, I told her about my job. I talked about how I didn't know what I was getting into necessarily, but I had heard different things, so I had a starting point. Truth be told, I knew names, but only a few of the people in the building.

It can be just as hard for an adult as it is for a young person to make new friends. The secret I told her was that you have to understand just one key point about all people: ALL people are just trying to find their way in the world. Some are better at it than others. But the fact is that we are all alike in our humanness, and in our humanness none of us is perfect. As soon as you get that part of reality, it makes it a lot easier to talk to people.

I also shared that I was given a bag of Hershey Hugs from the teacher I work with. I often walk down the hallway on my way to make copies, and give handfuls of the candy out to people. Some of them I know better than others, but I think that everyone can use a hug now and then. Why not go up to people and hand them a chocolate hug and wish them a good day? If I were able to get to my building earlier, I might tend to go room to room and drop a hug on everyone's desk.

I may or may not ever be a part of the group that is already there, because some of them have worked together for years. But even so, how much better is it to smile and say hello or hand someone a chocolate hug, than to go through the halls worrying about fitting in? I explained to my daughter that it doesn't matter if I fit in. What matters is if I'm doing a good job and I'm bringing glory to God.

The way I figure it, if she goes to school and she smiles and talks to whomever she comes in contact with, and she is right with God, everything else will fall into place.

She said that if the Mayans were correct and the end of the world comes this year, high school isn't going to matter much. I told her that I don't believe that the Mayans were privy to when Jesus was going to come back and take us to Heaven. Even if they were, it's a much better use of her time to live each day as God has intended, than to worry about what anyone else thinks of her.

Section 4

Dear Mom,

Did you ever notice that the women in our family all had short hair after a certain age? I am a little afraid to grow my hair out, because it would go against the norm in my mind. I realize that I have short hair because I am lazy and I don't want to spend more than seven minutes fixing it in the morning, but why did everyone else have short hair? It's curious, don't you think?

My hands are starting to look like yours. Sometimes I think I am looking at your hands. Remember when the girls were born and you said they would be piano players because they had such long fingers? Well, Megan plays the piano. She also plays oboe and bassoon for the school band. You would be so proud. I guess those long fingers came in handy. Apparently she is like her mom and is full of a lot of hot air, too. Some days more than others, she has a look about her that reminds me of you. When her hair was longer (before she cut it and donated it), she looks a lot like you when you were young.

Daphne reminds me of you, too. She gets so mad at me, just like you did. When she gets carried away, I call her by your name. She hates it when I do that, but if the shoe fits... She likes to give me the silent treatment like you used to. You know how much I hate that. It is like she is disciplining me instead of the other way around. Is it further punishment if I just keep talking to her when she doesn't want to talk to me? I can't be sure.

Scotty is such a great kid; you would be so happy with that boy. We were both scared that I was having a boy, but God blessed us with a good one. I think Misty was disappointed that he turned out the way he did. He is so smart and active, but he doesn't break things or get muddy and do other wild boy things. He likes sports like his dad and likes to read like his mom. He has great hugs; you would love them.

That is all for now.

Love,

Heather

Question:
Is It OK Not to Shave Your Legs in the Winter?

A question as old as time. Do you agree?

Here is how I think of it. I do not live in an area that is warm in the winter. I am also quite cold in the winter. I think we should be allowed to relax in the winter and use the hair God gave us to keep warm. I hear you now, saying, "Ewww, gross!" Do you think Eve worried about shaving? Do not even get me started on her… again. If I am to be punished for an apple and have three cesarean sections, I think I should be allowed to keep warm in the winter by not shaving. Who besides your husband (who has promised in front of God and these witnesses to love you in good and bad, sickness and health) is going to see your legs in the winter, anyway?

I will tell you. The principal of the school, that's who. When you fall out on the sidewalk, on a day that the nurse isn't in the building you work in. That's who will see your hairy legs when you go in to the nurse's office to ask for a bandage. Yeah… not cool.

If you have your "yearly exam" in the winter, the doctor will see your legs. Good idea to shave then. You don't want to be "that woman" making the doctor feel like he/she has to be careful not to get cut on your jagged poky leg hairs.

And then there are dressing rooms. The lighting in a dressing room is magically designed to make you look fat. Do you really want the hair on your legs to be magnified under that lighting and in those mirrors? When you pass out from the shock of seeing your unshaven legs in that light, and security has to break the door down to get to you because a store worker heard a loud *thunk* and you are laying on the dressing room floor… you are going to wish you had shaved.

Shoe shopping. Unless you are shopping for boots or tennis shoes and not for heels (for your neighbor's/cousin's/best friend's wedding), you will be fine. If a special occasion is in your future and you need to dress up, with pantyhose, leg fur is not going to be the best look.

Two words: Spring break. Remember, if you are going to a place more tropical than your own home for spring break, and you have spent the winter growing your fur coat to keep warm, you may need heavy-duty razor to get through that. Two may be required. And have fun on your trip.

I'm sure there are other occasions to shave in the winter. I not sure any of them are adequate enough to get me to shave daily, but maybe there are enough to make it at least a weekly event.

Vaughn promised in front of God and the witnesses. Three cesareans later, he can give me this one.

Marketing Meeting

My daughter Daphne is a marketing genius, apparently. Right now, she has 814 followers on Instagram, and 1008 followers on Tumblr. I have a total of four pictures on Instagram. I don't even know what Tumblr is about. I don't know why we need either one of these websites. Can we not share pictures on Facebook?

There are so many social networks. How do you know which is which and what you are supposed to do on them? I have no idea. I did not grow up in the computer era. We didn't have computers or computer classes when I was in school. We didn't talk on social networks on a computer, and we didn't text. We used the telephone or went to someone's house if we wanted to talk to someone. We missed the boat with all of these things.

What do you share and what do you not share? I read in the book "Start" by Jon Acuff that he does very little on Facebook but uses his blog, Twitter and Pinterest. I happen to follow him on Facebook. If what he does there is considered very little, I have a LONG way to go in the social network arena.

Several years ago I grudgingly got a Facebook because my friend Christi thought we could talk there. We have free Verizon to Verizon minutes, so I wasn't quite sure why we needed it, but I got it anyway. I have had a blog for a few years because another friend told me I should have one, so I got one of those without fully understanding what it was either. I got a Twitter account, but at present I cannot think of who talked me into that one. I may have just wanted to see what one did when they tweeted. Apparently they do not turn into birds.

Now I have a Pinterest account that makes me feel bad. I should be more crafty, and I don't have waterfront property with a perfect wardrobe. Instagram I don't get. Why do I need it, when I can take pictures just fine with the camera on my phone — or, here's a crazy thought — a camera? I have taken four pictures, and one of them is of a cupcake that looks like a reindeer.

I sat down with Daphne one day and asked her if she had any ideas to get more people reading. She went to my Facebook author page and started checking out all of my settings. Her first idea was to change the settings so that my target audience is people who want to follow pages that talk about drinking. I had to explain to her that I don't talk about drinking, so it would be misleading, and they would leave as soon as they showed up. She then thought I should change the language to strong so people could use all sorts of foul language on my page. I shot that idea down, too. She then insisted on being the administrator on the page. (She is not the administrator on the page.)

I am not sure if she doesn't know how to help me, or if she didn't think I was serious. While I do enjoy an occasional slushy wine, I do not write about drinking. I am not going to change my personality or my target audience for numbers. I suppose at some point, she may decide to help me with her social media marketing expertise.

It didn't occur to me when it all began that I was going to have to learn to Tweet, craft, take expert pictures, cook, and put #hashtags in front of my words and runthemtogether. But apparently Daphne is an expert. I have challenged her to come up with ideas that pertain to what I do.

So if you follow me on Facebook or Twitter or anything of that sort, and I suddenly start looking like I have a clue as to what I am doing, you can take that to mean that my marketing genius got serious about teaching me, and I even listened.

Sweet or Mean?

If you spend any time on Facebook, you will find that people take all kinds of quizzes and play all kinds of games. They will then send you requests wanting you to take the same quizzes and play the same games.

I have gotten several requests recently, requesting that I take a quiz that will determine if I am sweet or mean. Seriously? Do people really need to take a quiz to determine that? Can one not tell if they are sweet or mean? What can one be doing wrong that they need a quiz to determine their mood?

There is also a quiz that will tell you your true age. What do they mean their true age? Is it a calculator? Is it for people who are bad at math or have forgotten how old they truly are? Out of sheer curiosity, I took this quiz. It said I was sixteen. I think their calculations may be off.

There are farm games, cooking games, and animal games. There are gem games, fruit games, bubble games, and candy games. I have played a few of these games. It was ridiculous. I'm a suburb girl. I think chicken comes from the freezer section at the grocery store and vegetables either come from the freezer section or in cans. I've never lived on a farm, so I didn't understand the upkeep required. I have cats because they are low maintenance. I cook only with detailed instructions to tell me what to do. It was a lot of pressure to keep the farms going and the animals alive, along with real life, so I quit playing. You cannot pet an animal on the internet anyway.

I play the old-school Freecell and Spider solitaire when I am supposed to be writing, reading or relaxing. I never ask anyone to play any of these games. I don't take quizzes (except the one). I can pretty much tell by my children's reaction to me if I'm sweet or mean today. I can also tell you how old I am because my children remind me almost daily. I know which eighties movie best describes me, but I'm not telling. I'll let you figure that one out on your own.

So are you sweet or mean today? I'll give you a clue: you can always tell if people are running in the other direction when you're walking toward them.

Shape Up or Ship Out

In 2008, I went on a journey to get in shape. I lost about sixty pounds. I kept that weight off for about three years, and then the weight started creeping back on after I stopped exercising and went back to work. What can I say? I can only focus on one thing at a time.

This year my husband and I are trying to lose weight together. Our oldest daughter is with us in this quest also. Yesterday we had yet another snow day, so we were all home. The girls started getting far too aggressive with each other, so I sent the oldest to get on the treadmill to work off some aggression.

She did level two, which is an improvement from the level one that she usually saunters through. While she was walking, she kept telling me how much she hated me. So I started giving her a hard time for saying that, when she was only on level two.

This morning I couldn't talk myself out of getting on the treadmill, which is what I normally do. The girls had to be somewhere early and so I was up with time to kill before having to get ready for my son's basketball game.

I got on the treadmill and started on level three. When it started, I thought to myself, "This isn't so bad. I have no idea what her problem was with level two."

Below are the things that passed through my mind as I continued.

1. Wow, this is a little harder than I remember.
2. Speed four is really fast.
3. Incline ten? Really? I don't want to climb Mount Rushmore; I just wanted to get on the treadmill and burn some calories.
4. I haven't gone a mile yet? This thing might be broken; I think I've gone at least three miles.
5. Wow… my head is starting to hurt.
6. If I trip and fall off, can my ten-year-old get me up?
7. My spine may be out of line.
8. Climbing a mountain again, huh? Don't they give you ropes to hold onto when you climb mountains?
9. I think my head may explode. I think I have a brain tumor. That cannot be a good sign.
10. It could be a blood clot. It can't be in my legs, because they are now rubber, so it could have traveled to my head.

When my husband got up, he and asked me how I was doing. I told him I was pretty sure I was going to die. He asked me what level I was on. I told him three. He shook his head, chuckled, and walked away. He didn't know about the blood clot in my head.

When I got off the treadmill, the room started spinning. I felt like I was walking through a fun house.

So the moral of the story is this: Don't laugh at the daughter who can do level two without passing out, when you do level three and feel like you might be dying. Don't laugh at those who do the work you should be doing – or karma will give you a headache. I think that's going to be a popular phrase soon.

Well played karma, well played.

Keeping it Real

"Why do you always keep it real with us?" That is the question that my oldest likes to ask me.

As you can guess, I am a straight shooter. I do not believe that it does them any service to hold back or sugarcoat. This applies to anything that comes up, usually. I do censor quite a bit if the topic is uncomfortable, but I do tell them what I think.

I tell them what friends of theirs I like, and which I don't think are good for them. I tell them when they are being ridiculous. I tell them when they are being mean, ungrateful, selfish, and immature. The way I see it, they need to know, so they can change the behavior.

I like to tell the truth. I also like to get my money's worth. So when my daughter doesn't wash her face at night (using the hundred dollars' worth of skin care that I bought for her to use to take care of herself), it doesn't go over well. I don't mind buying things that they will use and that are designed to help them. But I am not about to spend a fortune on something that they "need" and have them not use it. I am going to tell them how I feel about it.

In this instance, I usually say, "Go do your face."

She usually responds with "No, I am tired. I don't want to."

To which I respond with, "Well, I am not really concerned with your exhaustion at this point, since you have spent at least the last hour sitting/laying on your butt and not moving. So get up off your rear end and go take care of yourself, so you don't have skin issues later."

This approach doesn't always work, as much as it makes her mad. I have tried simply asking her to take care of herself, but that doesn't work either, because it just makes her think that I am going soft and she doesn't need to listen (or do what I ask). Why she doesn't seem to care about taking care of her wellbeing is beyond me. The only thing I can figure is that the friends she has on the television cannot see her, so it doesn't matter.

This same daughter likes to try and kick me out of her room, if I go in to tell her she needs to do something other than what she is doing. This is met with a reality check. The reality check goes something like this: "I will not get out of your room, as I own this room. It is in my house and I have paid for ninety-nine percent of what this room holds. I even paid the doctors to deliver you. Therefore, I suggest you remember your manners, young lady. You are not allowed to kick me out of a room *I own*."

Then she tells me how it is her room... so I start doing some math as to how much rent is so she can pay for her room. Only then would she have the right to kick me out of her room. She doesn't have a job other than her chores around here, and I don't pay well. I also like to remind her of what the Bible says about honoring her mother and father, and that by disrespecting me, she is disrespecting God's word.

We have also had the "talk" with the girls. Well, my husband did most of the talking, and I sat there and added in details where they were needed, but mostly I was there for moral support. He is in the medical field. I felt we should be clinical about it. Not to mention that it makes me incredibly uncomfortable. (I now understand why my mother never had the "talk" with me).

We informed them that sex is between a husband and wife, and that we believe that you should wait until marriage to have it. Apparently we stressed this point so much, that this is how babies are made, that they didn't think it was even possible to do the act until you were married. When kids in their school showed up pregnant out of wedlock, they were thrown for a loop.

Plus, the idea of sex kind of grossed them out at that time. So I had to talk to them again about how it was possible for teenagers to get pregnant. The question was, "Why would anyone even want to do that?"

I replied "Well…because it is fun and it feels good?" This mortified them. Keep in mind, they were not yet in high school at this point, and while they still believe it is unfathomable that people at their age could be doing that (a fact that I thank God for every day), they no longer ask me about it, because apparently my answer was more "real" than what they were looking for.

Of course, being married to a pharmacist who doesn't believe in drugs helps with the "don't do drugs" conversation as well. If you cough up a lung, we will give you some cough medicine. If you have a fever, we will give you something for that. We just don't go running to the doctor for every little thing, and we don't give you medicine for the slightest malady. The main things I like to keep on hand are antacids and Midol. After that, you are pretty much going to have to have some chicken noodle soup, tea, or a wet washcloth (the best remedy outside of a bandage with a cartoon character on it).

We don't want to teach our children that medicine is bad, but we have expressed to them that some drugs are bad, and that even good drugs that are used improperly can be bad. Addicts became addicts because they took prescription drugs too far, simply because it made them feel good. Life is hard; you don't need to feel invincible. You only need to feel loved. With God you can do all things; not so much with drugs.

I complement my children when they do well. I tell them they are loved, but I also tell them when they make mistakes. I think that it is important not to build them up so they think they are perfect. Perfection is unattainable. You can strive for it every day, but there has only ever been one perfect person on earth and they are not it. I'm certainly not, either. Jesus is the only perfect person ever to walk the earth. They are creations of God and they need to see their flaws and strive to seek His will for their lives. Only God can make them perfect. So I keep it real. Shouldn't we all?

Changing the View

There is a room in our house that has changed titles several times in the course of the thirteen years that we have lived there. When we moved in, it was the dining room. When we moved in our girls were four and three, and the dining room had carpet and white walls. Clearly not the best choice of rooms to feed them in, or leave them unsupervised with crayons (yes, they "redecorated" for me).

The room changed into my mother's bedroom, when my mother was diagnosed with stage four lung cancer. First, it held a full size bed and dresser, then a hospital bed and dresser. Once she passed, the room had to change again. It became the playroom for the kids. But it didn't have any actual doors to hide the mess, so it became quite an eyesore. (When mother was in that room, we had curtains in the doorways.)

It then became an office ... that needed help. We had the downstairs redecorated not long after my mom passed. I was struggling to live in my house. I couldn't look in that room without feeling the weight of the world on me. At that time, I gave my husband three options.

    1. Move to Florida.

    2. Move to another house in the area.

    3. Redecorate our house so that it was different enough for me to live there comfortably, but still nice enough that I wouldn't want to leave.

He chose option three.

We enlisted professional help to get everything looking nice. Our decorator helped us pick out what would go into the room, but then never came back to show us where to put our things.

The office furniture just got moved, for the third time since the redecorating. The two previous times my desk has faced a wall. It is hard to be creative when all you have to look at is a wall. This last time, I could look out the window, at the shed. I suppose I could have admired the shed doors I built two summers ago and still haven't painted, but that was getting old too. When you spend your time plugged into your iTunes library, chewing gum while you write, it makes it easier for people to sneak up on you too.

I needed a change of view. One day when my husband was working, the girls were studying, and the boy was off playing with friends, I made a huge mess. I took all the stuff and moved it into the living room to make it easier to move the furniture around, then I rearranged the furniture. Then I did something crazy. I moved my desk around, so it faced the family room. Now from my desk, I can see my mother's wedding picture, and pictures of my grandmothers. I can see two of my children's plaster handprints, and the footprint of the other one. If I look into the living room, I can see the plaque above my daughter's piano that has Jeremiah 29:11 on it.

I wrote three blog posts in two days after I moved everything around.

Sometimes we need a change of view. Sometimes we need a change of routine. Sometimes we need an attitude change. I changed my view, felt better about the room, and felt better in general. My creativity was restored, just because I wasn't staring at a wall.

How many times do we just get tired of staring at the wall we have run into? Have you hit a brick wall with your faith? Have you hit a brick wall with your life? What can you do to change your view? Rearrange the furniture? Rearrange the roadblocks in your heart?

I have to be honest here. This time, I rearranged the furniture, and it seemed to help me. This time, however, is not every time. When

I am involved in a Bible study with a group of ladies to hold me accountable, I am more apt to stay on track, and feel closer to God. I feel like things are going to be OK, even if they aren't perfect.

God is never stagnant. He doesn't hit a brick wall. He loves us, even when we feel like we are going nowhere, and feel weak. 2 Corinthians 12: 8-10 says: "Three times I pleaded with the Lord to take it away from me. But he said to me, 'My grace is sufficient for you, for my power is made perfect in weakness.' Therefore I will boast all the more gladly about my weaknesses, so that Christ's power may rest on me. [1] That is why, for Christ's sake, I delight in weaknesses, in insults, in hardships, in persecutions, in difficulties. For when I am weak, then I am strong."

Did you catch that? Even when we are weak, we are strong. Even when we fall short, hit a brick wall, feel stuck, even when we aren't perfect (which we will never be because it is unattainable), His grace is sufficient for us.

So rearrange some furniture. Take down some roadblocks or brick walls around your heart and feel God's perfection in your life. Change your view.

The Birds & the Bees

While on vacation this year, I was minding my own business, walking through a patch of palm trees, when all of a sudden -- poo. On my eye, and around my eye. Not in my hair, nowhere near my clothes, or shoes.

On. My. EYE! Seriously!

I went to the restroom and washed my eye. Then I washed it two more times, and flushed it all out until I finally felt like I wasn't going to hyperventilate. The rest of the day all I could think of was bird flu. You don't just bounce right back when a bird poos on your eye.

Today, I went out to the shed to get the lawn mower out. When I opened the door, I noticed a couple of small bee hives attached to the inside of the door. I didn't concern myself too much with them, because I didn't intend on bothering them. I figured they would leave me alone.

Oh, no. I no sooner started pulling out the mower out when one of the bees stings me on the back of the neck.

On the back of my neck in case you missed the where. Do you know what is in your neck? All sorts of things that keep you alive, like blood and spinal fluid and a spine. That is what is in your neck.

I hadn't been stung by a bee since childhood. The pain from a bee sting gets worse before it gets better. I went inside and grabbed ice and called my mother-in-law, who is a nurse, to ask her what else to do. Apparently ice and baking soda is the magic cure. I wrapped a paper towel around ice, using a scarf to keep it there. After the allotted time of 30 minutes, to make sure I didn't have a reaction, I mowed the yard.

I am not pleased with flying animals anymore. Birds no longer intrigue me with their beautiful flight. I want to learn how to shoot them out of the air. That is where I'm at with birds. After my oldest daughter and I went to run some errands one day, the yard was full of birds. I told her to run over them with the car. She didn't. She has never been pooed on. I may get over it... I may not.

As far as bees go, I've decided to eat a lot of honey. I may eat honey every single day for the rest of my life. Those bees now work for me. My husband has instructions to take care of those hives and the bees that live in them. I am not going be scared to get in the shed.

These flying creatures apparently have a problem with me. I used to be so enamored with their flight. I used to have dreams of flying. Now I only want to fly in an airplane. I don't get pooed on in airplanes. I don't get stung on the back of the neck, near vital parts, on airplanes.

These instances have confirmed what I have always known about myself. I'm not outdoorsy. I will never find pleasure in camping. I don't want to go bird watching. I don't want to take up bee-keeping. That is for the birds (pun intended). No. No. No. Those flying creatures cannot be trusted.

They serve a purpose, I'm sure. I am pretty sure their purpose is not to poo on my eye or sting me on the back of the neck, however.

When I asked my mother about the birds and the bees as a teenager, do you know what she told me? Bees sting and birds poo on cars. Well, she got it partly right. Apparently they like eyes, too.

Boundaries

I find myself troubled by the television shows that are being made for the target audience of teenagers. As the mother of two teenage girls, I will not allow them to watch quite a bit of "regular" TV. They also choose not to watch a lot of what is being offered, thank goodness, preferring a number of shows from my childhood. Currently, "The Facts of Life" is huge in my house.

What is with the writers for today's teens? There are three shows on now, that I can think of, about teen pregnancy. When I was in seventh grade, I was one of the younger kids in my class, at twelve. A girl in my class got pregnant and had a baby. Take a minute and wrap your mind around that. I'll wait.

I was just naïve enough at that age to not fully understand how that was possible. I didn't get sex education until health class in high school. The only thing my mother ever told me about sex was when I was in high school. When I told her that I thought it was time we had "the talk, you know, the birds and the bees? The facts of life?" this is what she told me: Bees sting, birds poo on cars and those are the facts of life. So suffice to say, I got sex education from health class, the lunchroom at school, and the movie "Mischief."

As a parent to two teenage daughters, we have had many talks with our girls. We started much earlier than my mother did, and obviously have given them information and expanded on it as they were older and able to understand more.

When I was growing up, teenage pregnancy was frowned upon; socially unacceptable. I knew a girl who went to a private school and got pregnant, and she wasn't allowed to return. She had to take her classes at home and only go into school for tests. Pregnancy was not something to strive for. We didn't put those girls on television, give them money, and make them out to be role models simply because they learned how to change a diaper and take chemistry at the same time. Obviously they had at least one form of chemistry figured out already.

What I want to know is, where are the boundaries? When did it become socially acceptable to not discipline our kids, or to teach them right from wrong? I get that sometimes kids are going to have sex, no matter what you have taught them at home. I get that kids do stupid things and sometimes it is no fault of the parents. But I have seen parents get their young teen's pictures taken with their boyfriend or girlfriend, like an engagement picture.

My girls have classmates that aren't old enough to drive cars, but they are allowed to date. What is the rush? This is the twenty-first century. It is not the 1800s when they needed to get married at thirteen, lest they be a burden to their family. Their parents let them walk around showing as much cleavage as a Victoria's Secret model, with pants so tight and low that they leave nothing to the imagination. No one dresses like they have a secret anymore.

We grew up with curfews and discipline, and respect for the older generation was a given. Family values were at the heart of the television shows we watched. Today, while walking down the hallway, I heard third graders talking about the movie "Paranormal Activity" and other scary movies they had seen. I shook my head and wondered what has happened to the world we live in. I still wonder how much worse things are going to get when we are glorifying teenage pregnancy, the news reports mostly bad news because that will get viewers (either that, or we have no good news to report), and I fear for my kids and their kids' futures.

What has happened to our world when kids want to get emancipated, a word they heard on television, when they don't like the rules of the house? What has happened to the world when they say they will call child services if you discipline them? I used to get my butt beat; I turned out fine. If I had talked to my mother the way kids talk to their mothers today, I wouldn't have any teeth left that were my own. I tell my kids when they backtalk me, that if their grandmother were alive they would be on the floor looking for their behinds, and possibly some of their teeth. That is a fact.

I was a smart-mouth kid, so of course it stands to reason that my biggest pet peeve is backtalk and blatant disrespect. If my children tell me they want to get emancipated, or they want to call child services because I grounded them and took their electronics away, I will dial the phone for them and help them pack.

I love my kids more than anything you can imagine. But I will not go against what God teaches for them. I will not teach them that they can be a burden to society and that they don't have to work for anything. I will not glorify their mistakes. I will teach them right from wrong. I will tell them when they are wrong, and at the same time, I will tell them how very much I love them.

But I will not teach them that love is fleeting, and that if it doesn't work out being married, they can just get out of it and move on. Marriage is forever. The vows are taken in front of God. If one of you makes a mistake, you need to ask God to heal what is broken, and not dissolve the marriage because of anger and hurt. God can heal relationships. God can help them in any situation. But they need to ask God, before putting themselves into situations that can potentially harm them, instead of thinking they may get their own television show out of it.

Family values: that is what I want my children to get from the television shows I allow them to watch, and from me. I have made my share of mistakes, and so will my kids. But I refuse to allow them to make light of what truly matters.

God help our world. Lead us back to what matters and help us to seek your guidance in all things.

Sweating Like a Turkey the Week Before Thanksgiving

The problem is this... I am afraid of mowing the ditch in front of my yard with the riding lawn mower. This is the reason why I decided that push-mowing the ditch was a good idea.

Don't get me wrong—I love the riding lawn mower. It doesn't go especially fast, ever since I tipped it. (Don't worry, I'm fine. I rolled out of the way). This is how it happened.

Not long after we got the mower, I was out mowing, like good landscape artists do, and I realized I had forgotten to get the swings out of the way on the swing set. The appropriate response to this situation would be to stop the mower, get off of the mower, move the swings, get back on the mower, and continue. I didn't choose that option. No.

The option I chose was to stay on the mower and attempt to lean forward to get each of the swings out of the way, as I passed through. You see where this is going, right? The swing got caught on the rather large gear shift (which is much larger than our old mower) and the mower started going up, up, up and over backwards. I did what any idiot of my caliber would do, jumped off and rolled. Fortunately, the mower then turned itself off, but not before it was stuck in the dirt, upside down, with its rather large gear shift buried into the lawn a few inches.

You can imagine how well this went over with my husband. We had had this mower for about three weeks. I went in, shaking, with my tail between my legs to explain what I had done. But he knew I was an idiot when he married me. He was able to get the jack from the car to get it out of the dirt.

I was then banned from all mowing for a year, and only allowed to mow again IF I promised to either move the swings before mowing, or just go around the swing set in the future. I did, and I have been happily mowing ever since. Except for the ditch. I still avoid the ditch like the bubonic plague. Any area that slants or tilts makes me shifty. I can't do it. I have flashbacks. But I realized that my hard-working husband, who conquers this area with the riding mower without incident (unlike me), wasn't going to be able to get to mowing the ditch. So I decided to get the push mower out and take care of it.

I am a bit out of shape. This is an especially sad fact, as I was once in very good shape. I haven't figured out how to manage my time effectively to work out anymore, between work and family and my excellent skills at procrastinating. It's a problem that became evident as I was push-mowing said ditch.

It is hot in the summer. Now, I love summer. I am normally quite cold and I don't thaw out till it's about 75 degrees. Summer is a welcomed blessing. Also, I don't normally sweat a lot. I was push mowing that ditch and sweating more than a turkey the day before Thanksgiving. I may only be able to eat Thanksgiving dinner-sized meals now because of the amount I sweated while mowing that ditch.

You may ask yourself, how important is the ditch, really? It's right by the road, and people could park there and push the grass down. They don't usually, but it could happen. If it were up to me, I would just pave it. We are about to have another driver in the house; we could use the extra parking space. Then the parking for parties or my un-mowed ditch would never be a problem.

The neighbors' complaints about my singing and dancing while I mow would go down, since there would be less area to do. (I could still sing in the car and dance behind the privacy fence when the music demands). Or I could just keep mowing the ditch with the push mower, then work my way up to mowing the entire front yard, until I could do the entire yard. Why, I could be skinny and fit in no time at all!

I should give this some serious thought… but after Thanksgiving.

Self-Control

I once read and have heard that if you have some self-control, then you shouldn't have any trouble losing weight. That may be the most ridiculous thing I have ever heard. If I had self-control, I wouldn't need to lose weight in the first place.

In fact, if everyone had self-control, then obesity would cease to exist. Americans everywhere would be fit and have a BMI of like, ten, because everyone would be a ten. That is how much I know about BMI, because I don't even know if that is a good or bad number. Math being my strongest subject and all, the BMI is not something I really pay attention to. Obviously, or I wouldn't be here — five years out from having lost fifty-five pounds and currently in need to lose thirty more to weigh what my driver's license says I weigh. I just really like ice cream, and pizza, and chocolate, and well... sitting down. My fingers get exercise as I type; surely that counts for something, right?

As I think about self-control, I am pretty sure that if we as a country had that, no one would ever be in debt, and the national debt would be a national surplus. Living within one's means is not only smart: it's Biblical. Living in a society that condones and promotes borrowing from Peter to pay Paul, and the "need" for credit, does nothing to help with self-control. All it does is dig deeper holes and creates more problems for the immediate-satisfaction society that we find ourselves in. This is scary. If you look around at how it is for us, imagine what it is going to be like for our children. Forget about leaving a legacy. You are going to leave them with a headache and the need for a large shovel so they can dig themselves out of the mess that you leave them with.

Money is just one example. Self-control would eliminate teenage pregnancy, I'm pretty sure. Teenage boys everywhere just fell over at the thought of having to wait until marriage. (Mothers everywhere just did a backflip and a hallelujah). I remember being a teenager. I remember the hormones. I still have them; they just are doing different things. They are busy with the production of gray hair and placing random eyebrow hairs in places like the middle of my nose. You gain some sense of self-control when you have three kids and two of them are teenagers. You see what they turn into, not just what they start out as.

If more people had self-control, everyone would get along. People wouldn't argue, because they would be busy biting their tongues. I think that there definitely would be fewer people getting upset on social media sites. Conversations over the computer make it hard to judge a person's tone, therefore making it hard to tell when there is sarcasm, or joking. This leads to more disagreements, and that is just silly. If you know someone in person who is a jokester or that they are sarcastic, then most likely they are that way on the site you are socializing with them on. If you don't get upset at them in person, why get upset on the computer?

Let me help you here. If you are upset with me for something that I say on a social media site, you need to relax. I am not out to get you or upset you. I am likely joking and assume (which gets many like me in trouble) that you can take a joke. I tend to joke more with people I like too, so if I like you, just be prepared for it.

Facebook and other social media sites would be less populated if people had more self-control. Seriously, it's like a drug. You just *have* to see what everyone's doing; if you don't, you are missing stuff. What are they going to have for dinner tonight? Will they have the roast beef or will they go with the chili? Are their kids still perfect? Did they get their bunions removed? Do they have gas?

Are they still fighting that cold that everyone has? Are they cold? Are they hot? Are they hungry? Are they allergic to cheese? Mr. Zuckerberg became a very rich man banking on our lack of self-control, as did Papa John, Little Caesar's and every other pizza place.

People post everything on these sites. Let me save you some time, in case you are one of the people who is not on social media. We ordered pizza. My kids are normal and not perfect. I don't have bunions, but I might have gas later (because we had pizza for dinner), I still have the cold but it's getting better, I'm comfortable, I'm not hungry, I love cheese. Now that we got that out of the way, we don't have to head over to Facebook for at least another twenty minutes.

I am sure that I could come up with several other examples. But what could we do better? With some self-control, we could *be* better; we would read more, we would love more, we would care more, we would share more, we would spend some more time with God and less time on the things we think are more important.

I'm not sure how well I am doing in this department, as far as what God thinks. But I think He would say that I need to take better care of myself, spend less time worrying about what other people think, and worry more about what He thinks. I'm sure I should spend more time with Him, more time with those that love me most, and less time with people I may upset on a social media site.

Friends talk things out and don't just "unfriend" you. God doesn't defriend. He loves at all times, in all circumstances, and He can teach us all we need to know about self-control.

Dust Bunnies - Ya Gotta Love 'Em

I read somewhere that "dust gives a home a warm, fuzzy feeling." If I'm being truthful, I probably read that on Facebook or Pinterest.

I was thinking of this statement as we spent our Labor Day weekend cleaning our home. I mean, serious cleaning. We emptied out bedrooms and swept, dusted, and rearranged. We carried out bags of trash and things to give away. The bedrooms look great! Today, we were given an extra day off school, due to fog. With that extra time, we finished the last bedroom, then I proceeded to clean my office to the level of tolerable, and rearrange the man cave. When that was done, I mowed the yard.

The reason this all came about was that the level of dust in this house probably could have blanketed a third-world country.
The dust and cat hair under the beds alone was so bad; you would have thought we had a Yeti living here.

I'm not sure how this happens. We are relatively clean people. We sweep, but we sweep what we can see. Actually, my daughter sweeps; it's her chore. My son, who is nine, is in charge of dusting. That may be a clue in this mystery. I'm not even going to get into what may be happening in the bathrooms; I haven't gotten that far yet. My other daughter is in charge of cleaning those.

My job, aside from my day job of cooking all the food, and the running kids around, is laundry and mopping. The laundry gets done. The mopping is sketchy. I need to work on that. Or maybe I could trade with the boy and do the dusting, and try him out on the mopping? Hmm… I may be on to something here.

I read in a book once about a house that was self-cleaning. Imagine a self-cleaning house. It probably involves some technology that I won't figure out. Just this year, we bought a stove with a self-cleaning oven, and I don't know how to use it yet.

(I will tell you that I am a huge fan of the flat-top cook stove. That is also my job to clean, but it is a breeze compared to the old stove. It is also stainless steel, and I'm pretty sure it is the sexiest kitchen appliance around. That was my comment to my husband when it was delivered: "That is the sexiest appliance I've ever seen." So I don't get out much; sue me.)

It feels so nice when the house is clean, don't you think? I try to keep things clean, but inevitably I will find a cobweb or some dust somewhere that I missed. Something always happens and the clean house isn't so clean anymore. The cats will come in and shed all over the freshly-swept carpet. Kids tromp through the house with their friends, and in just moments, leave a trail of dirty dishes, food wrappers, half-opened backpacks, and Legos in their wake.

I think it feels that way with life sometimes, too. You are going along just fine, then there is some dust or a cobweb that happens to dirty things up. As often as I try to clean up my soul, I can't get it ever completely done. Just like I can clean the house and it just gets dirty again, I can attend worship and listen to worship music, but I cannot get rid of the cobwebs and dust in my soul; not forever. Only God can do that.

Only when we give ourselves over to Him completely can we feel truly cleaned up and free. I'm so glad I can count on my God to cover that part. Because the cat just shed on the floor again, and I have my hands full.

How Much Protection Do We Really Need?

I was shopping recently and I had to go down an aisle that most men avoid like the plague – you know, the "feminine hygiene supplies." As I looked at the "levels of protection" offered by the various brands, it struck me that it's good to have choices. There is light, for those who don't require much protection at all, regular for an average amount, and super for those who require a bit more help. Now I'm not going to get into what those things specifically protect you against. But I will tell you that I realized that the protection I needed, they don't offer.

I have an active imagination. That comes in handy when you are a writer. It also comes in handy when you live in a small town. Unfortunately, that also means that I spend a lot of time thinking about what-ifs. For instance, I have the weather radar up on the internet at all times. What if a storm comes and throws the internet out and I can't get my email? One of the main reasons I got a smart phone was for the sole purpose of following storms on the weather radar, when the power is out. I do trust in the Lord to protect me, but if He has given us the technology to follow weather patterns, shouldn't I have that information, so I can protect my family?

I need the protection that only God can provide. I need a "batten down the hatches, this boat is going for a ride, and a storm is coming" kind of protection. "The captain of the boat is not driving, he is partying on the Lido Deck" kind of protection. I want Jesus to walk on the water and calm the seas. I want Him to call me out to the water, then walk me to dry land. I want THAT kind of protection. I want to sit in my heavenly Father's arms, give him all of my insecurities and fears, and have him show me the steps to take. I want to know for certain that I am doing what He has called me to do, not what I think He wants.

What is more protection—being in the know, or not knowing? We keep things from our children to protect them. As adults, we prefer to know. If there is a train coming down the track, I want to know about it. Then I can make informed decisions. If I need to seek shelter in the neighbor's basement, I want to know. If there is something else I should be doing and I'm not, I want to know that, too. Like I said, I have an active imagination. I can imagine that God wants many things. What I want, is for God to tell me the plan.

What is your level of protection? Are you a light? Do you have it all under control; you just need a little coverage? Are you a regular? Do you have it mostly under control but need some general assistance? Or are you a super? Are you bordering on out-of-control?

Or are you like me? You need a level of protection and comfort that they don't sell at the store. The hatches need to be manned, and you can't make it on your own.

We are all completely off balance; broken, and very much in need of our Father. At one time or another, we all need the kind of protection that can only be given by the Father. Which level do you seek?

Pharmacist's Wife

My husband and I have been together at this point longer than we were apart in life. We met when I was just seventeen years old, and we went to senior prom together. I had seventeen years without him, and now I've had more than seventeen years with him. We've had a lot of plans and a lot of love. We've had good times and bad times. Times when we were mad about each other and times we were mad at each other.

I know what my husband does for a living. I was there when he went to college. I was there when he wasn't sure he was going to get in to pharmacy school. I was there when he did, and when he graduated.

I was reminded by two different people at work recently what my husband does for a living. I wasn't quite sure what to make of it. While I am a pharmacist's wife, I guess I never thought of that as my identity. More than that, I never thought that what my husband did for a living diminished what I did... until now. Then I got mad.

I didn't get mad at the people really, but the idea that what I did was less important made me angry. Because I am really happy. I am downright content in my life, but I'm content because of who I get to spend it with. Then I thought maybe the attack I felt wasn't because of him so much, as me.

I had a conversation with my husband about it. My goal in life was always to blend in. I never really wanted to draw attention to myself. Some people may dream of standing out in a crowd and being awesome. I didn't then and I don't now dream of being awesome. I dream of blending and sitting in peace on my white couch watching The History Channel with my pink laptop on my lap and playing FreeCell. I like doing what I do at my job. I like being in my house with my family. I had a crappy childhood and I just wanted a normal life, which is what we have. I'm good; I have nothing else I want to aspire to.

Or do I?

Now I have to go and be awesome in my own right, so people won't think I'm just some loser who lucked out and married a pharmacist. What is wrong with mediocre or average? I'll tell you what is wrong with it. It isn't awesome. The trouble is that I have no idea how to be awesome. Also, when you start trying to be awesome, people start acting weird around you, which has happened to me.

When my first book came out, I wasn't actually trying to be awesome. I enjoy writing, so I wrote. As it turns out, someone read my writing and thought it should be published. While I was excited and thought it was quite cool, I didn't think that made me awesome. I thought that made me lucky.

It's when you start working on another book, and start talking about speaking in public, is when things get weird. You get a different vibe from people. Maybe I've become some form of awesome without realizing it. I don't see it. I spend far more time seeing myself as I once was, instead of seeing myself as I am, or as I am becoming.

The thing about being awesome is that it is what God wants for each of us. He wants to give us far more that we can dream up or imagine. If you already tend to dream big, dreaming even bigger is not easy to do. I tend to dream big. But then I say, "That won't happen though, so I will settle for..." I don't know why I do that, other than the fact that I guess I don't believe I deserve the biggest dreams.

But what if I was? What if I just let go, and let God take me where he wants to and realize it's not about me? I don't have to be awesome. That pressure really isn't on me. I only have to be a willing participant, and let God show his awesomeness *through* me. When I think of it like that, I feel better about it. I feel better about most things when I take me out of it.

I am a pharmacist's wife. I am also a mother to three great kids, a kindergarten aide, and a writer for God. Maybe that's pretty awesome after all.

Section 5

Dear Mom,

Today is your birthday. You would have been sixty-one today. Crazy to think that this is another year we won't be celebrating your birthday.

Things are getting better. I can get through every holiday like a trooper now. It's your birthday and mine that get me every time. How is it that February 25 is here and you are not? If you were here, we would go to Texas Roadhouse for your birthday dinner. I would have made you a white cake with peanut butter icing. What would you have asked for?

My heart hurts today. I feel like I'm being ripped in two. I think about all that has happened that you weren't here for. I learned how to make jewelry and you loved jewelry. Are you mad that you didn't benefit from that? Do you even know that now that you are in Heaven, or are you so busy you haven't noticed what has been going on?

I started writing. I'm not sure that I am good at it. I suppose that is subjective, but I do enjoy it. Your oldest grandchild is starting to drive; your second is going to start driver's ed in the summer; the baby is ten and he has good hair. You would be so proud of them.

Today I find myself in another battle. The voices that haunt me are back for the day. "It is your fault." "You didn't fight hard enough." "Did you really do everything that you could have?" "What if you did this or what if you had done that?" "You just gave up. You gave up and now she is gone."

They persist with their accusations and it tears me apart. Eventually reason comes into play and I realize what is happening. I suppose I am a slow learner, or after almost nine years I would be able to shut them down faster.

I did not then and I do not now have the power to save anyone. While I took on the responsibility to take care of you alone, I was not then and am not now an oncologist, nor am I God. Your life, just as mine, was in God's hands and his hands alone. I know that God has a plan to bring beauty from these ashes. I revisit those last days sadly, and then I remember that even at the end, God was there. He sent his son to stand at the foot of your bed and take you home. I know that. I was there, I felt his presence.

I know you are home. I know you are having a wonderful birthday in the presence of our Lord. I know all of these things and I am so sad I am missing the party. I can only imagine the kind of party that God would throw. I can only imagine the joy he felt that you came to know him and you were saved and are with him now. These thoughts bring me peace when I feel that I cannot hold on.

I keep asking God to keep me moving. I ask him to tell you how much I miss you and love you. Sometimes I just get so mad at you and I tell him that too. I didn't get all of my questions answered. I didn't learn everything I needed to from you. I can't bake like you could. I miss talking to you on the phone while I fix dinner. I miss shopping with you.
I miss arguing with you. I miss all of your expressions.

"What do you want to do now, kong?"

"Do you have to go poo poo in the pee pee potty or pee pee in the poo poo potty?" The kids still remember that one and they think it is so funny.

I walk through the shadows today, with the hope that tomorrow the sun will shine again. God brings the light to my weary soul. I know that he will bring me through this day like so many others.

I keep moving, because I have hope. Hope for tomorrow, hope for His plan for my life, hope that one day I will see you again. Hope that when July comes and it's my birthday, that God will bring me through that battle as well. This year we will be very busy. Busy is good. It means less time to dwell on things that I still have no control over. Then the light bulb goes on and the lesson is learned yet again.

I am not in control. I never have been, and that is such a relief. It relieves my soul to know I can go to my Father and lay down my sorrows and troubles at his feet. He will wipe my tears and pick me up again and we will go on with the journey he has for me. And somehow I think maybe you know that too, that maybe he fills you in.

Love until we meet again,

Heather

If They Don't Get Older in the Scrapbook, Does That Mean They Will Never Leave?

My daughter is a junior in high school this year. My time for getting her scrapbooks caught up is ticking away like the second hand on a clock. I may have to hire it done. I am not even sure you can do that. I just know that I am not getting it done. Part of me thinks if I don't get it done, then she will stay with me.

I'm not ready for her to go. Sure, there are days when I am more than ready to see what comes next for her, but she comes honestly by her fear of change. I am terrified to not have her here. How do you go from spending every minute with them, to sending them to school, and then to sending them away to school? Was this in the book we received at the hospital on the way home? I don't remember that section. You go from having them with you twenty-four hours a day, to not having them with you at all. By the time we were juniors in college, we didn't even go home for the summer any more. We just stayed at college and came home for major holidays. I can't decide if that was a blessing to our parents or if they struggled also.

My freshman went away to an honor band weekend, and I was lost. I kept thinking that a part of my being was missing. There are supposed to be three of them. Not two. It was an odd thing to experience. This letting go business is hard.

We have started the journey of looking at prospective colleges with my oldest daughter. It is good that colleges provide food. If left to her own devices, she may starve. She wouldn't have a stove in her room, so she wouldn't be able to heat up a frozen pizza, and that is pretty much the only thing she can cook. She once tried to make a hot dog in the microwave and she cooked it for four minutes. It doesn't instill a lot of confidence when I think of her striking out on her own. I worried about her going to first grade and how she would carry her tray to the table without spilling it, and now I am worried about her food situation again.

I also worry about her safety, her study habits, and her ability to make friends. She is pretty quiet. If she and another quiet girl met, they could be good friends. But if they are both quiet, who is going to talk first?

I met the love of my life my senior year in high school. I had him for support during college. She hasn't started dating. This is a fact that I am happy about currently, because I have seen how some of those high school boys drive, and I have seen how she drives, and it is a frightening prospect. But it is one more person to write to; I would wait anxiously for the next letter. In the old days, you waited days for letters. Now with email, the wait is minutes. I suppose in that instance, the immediate gratification era has a point in its favor. With cell phones and email, we can be connected at all times. As it is, she calls me from her cell phone, from her room, when I am downstairs.

So if I never finish the scrapbook, will she never leave? Will I be holding her back from all she is yet to discover and be? Should I force her to do things she doesn't think she wants to do, just so she doesn't miss out on the experience? What will I do when I do let her go and she doesn't come home? Does that reflect well on my parenting, or poorly? Oh, how I wish I could ask my mother or grandmother about this.

Which part is easier—sending them to college or marrying them off? If I hit menopause when she does get married, can I request a winter wedding, so I won't sweat like a pig and stain the satin dress

I will be required to wear? Are teenagers so difficult to understand and deal with so it will be easier to see them go?

My questions are many, but the solutions are clear. When crunch time comes, the scrapbooks will be done, and I will let her go. She will spread her wings and she will leave the nest to see what the world has to offer and what God has planned for her. I just need to realize that while she is my child, she is also a child of God, and I don't own her. I have to hope that I have taught her something about the world and she knows how to get through life without being attached to my hip. God is as much with her as he is with me, and he will be with both of us during the next chapter.

After all, when I was in high school, I once caught the kitchen on fire making a PopTart for breakfast. All she did was overcook a hot dog, and the microwave is still in working order. She is already ahead and I turned out fine. Right?

Being the Bad Guy, or Why I Might Start Drinking

My oldest daughter signed up for classes for her senior year of high school. Her guidance counselor pulled her out of class and helped her get signed up, because we forgot to do it over the weekend. She was telling me about it when I picked her up from school.

She said, "Well, my guidance counselor knows what I want to do, so she was able to help me pick out my classes."

Almost cringing, I said, "What exactly did you tell her you wanted to do?"

"I told her I want to be a Mexican bullfighter."

This child is sixteen years old. I have no idea where she gets her smart mouth. I'm thinking, "Seriously? Can we not have a conversation? Did she really tell her counselor that, or did she tell her that as a joke? One can never tell. She can't take a joke, but can she tell one? If she did, would anyone get it?"

As calmly as I could, I said, "Really? A Mexican bullfighter, huh? It didn't occur to you to tell her you want to study journalism?"

She said, "No, I think I could be a good Mexican bullfighter. Or I might go into leaf blowing."

"First of all, three years of Spanish does not qualify you as a Mexican. And if you get into a fight with a bull, you will lose. You are completely full of it, so politics might be good for you. Or you might be a good lawyer. And leaf blowing? Did we pass someone just now that was blowing leaves?"

"Yes. But I think I could revolutionize the business. I think that leaf blowing could be very high-paying if I am the boss."

"Daphne, if you go into leaf blowing, you are going to be poor. Do you want to be poor?"

"Why would I be poor? Do they not make any money?"

"I am sure there are people that make money blowing leaves. However, you would not be one of them."

"Why not?"

"Because you hate going outside. You are the whitest girl I have ever seen! I have to practically bribe you and drag you out to get you to ride a bike or go swimming. I do not think that you would be successful in leaf blowing, because you have to go outside—where the leaves live—in order to blow them away!"

"Oh," she says.

She is the reason I think about drinking. OK, I don't really. But there are days when I think it may be a good option. Instead, I chew Trident gum. First, it is accepted by the ADA and it has Xylitol in it, so it's good for you... sort of. Also, blowing bubbles and popping them is a stress reducer. I think there have been studies. (I may have been the only subject in the study, but I am telling you it helps.) They got rid of my favorite flavor (sweet mint), but they came out with a new flavor called mint bliss, which is fabulous. Plus it helps to keep me from eating away my sorrows.

She did finally come clean and let me know she did tell the counselor what she really wants to study. However, when she started telling me what she signed up for, I got very concerned. She signed up for sociology and psychology. I took those classes in college, and I do not remember them being easy.

She said, "My guidance counselor told me they would be easy classes." I told her that of course her guidance counselor would think that they are easy; she is a social worker by trade. Lord of mercy. Bless my soul. The child is going to end me.

I said, "You need to bring up your GPA! Why didn't you sign up for something easy… like, ceramics?"

"I don't like to get dirty. I don't want to take ceramics," she said.

"But if you don't bring up your grades and get into a good college, the only jobs you will get will revolve around saying 'Would you like fries with that?', and if you end up having to be around raw meat, you will get grossed out and get fired. Ceramics would have at least given you a boost. You cannot get an A going to study hall."

I know it sounds like I am hard on her. But seriously, the kid needs to realize that in the fall, she will be applying to colleges, and she will be taking her SATs before then. She is not studying and preparing; she spends her time watching television and looking things up on the internet about old TV shows or Harry Potter. (When I introduced her to Harry Potter, I really had no idea what I was getting started. Also, I didn't know that by introducing her to the TV shows I watched as a child, that she would love them so much and become obsessed with them.)

How do you get them to understand? How am I going to adjust if she decides to not use her gifts as a writer and becomes a leaf blower who doesn't go outside to blow the leaves, but works in the office and tells them all how to do it? She won't even pull weeds in our yard.

She is comfortable at her desk. She wants to actually become a screenwriter. Of course, I wanted to be a fashion designer or fashion buyer, until I took a textiles class, and figured out I really just wanted to go shopping. I didn't care about knowing all of the different fabrics.

When do you stop being the bad guy? When do you stop being the stupid parents and become the best smartest people they know? That's where I want to be. Which is why I love working in kindergarten. You are a genius rock star when they are five and six years old. When they hit puberty, your I.Q. drops to just above, say, hedgehog. They think the cats are smarter than you are. I am thankful now for the twenty-four hours of labor (only to get taken upstairs for a c-section), because I use that.

"Twenty-four hours of labor and this is how you treat me! Seriously? Twenty-four hours of labor, only to be taken upstairs in a cold room and ripped open with a scalpel, only because you have to do things on your time? And this is how you treat me!"

Never gets old. Nope. Not even a little bit.

She wears me out. But oh, how I love her. In fact, part of me hopes she never leaves. I cannot imagine a day without her here arguing with me. I could do without her hating me most days, but at the end of the day she is one of my greatest treasures.

The Mind of Megan

My beautiful, talented, daughter Megan has a very active imagination. She also tends to get bored easily. For a couple months out of the year, she is very busy with getting ready for band competitions. When things slow down and she has nothing to look forward to or prepare for, she tends to, well… try to find something to entertain herself, and keep some of the attention flowing her way.

She also has very deep feelings for others. When her feelings get hurt, it takes her a long time to get over it. One of her friends hurt her recently, deciding that she doesn't want to be friends with Megan anymore. So that has been a sad loss. I tried to help, but since I became stupid (because of childbirth), I didn't make any progress. So I recommended that she see the guidance counselor at school to work through it.

She did that, but then she apparently liked the one-on-one so much, that she started going every day to talk. Which is interesting, because she has always been the child who has been content alone, doing her own thing. She isn't terribly concerned about what anyone else is doing. Then I got a call from the counselor's office yesterday, however, and the counselor said she wanted to talk to me about further counseling.

Now before you think I am a terrible mother, and that I wouldn't get my child the help that she must obviously need, let me explain what I know (that the counselor does not). When I got home from work, I noticed that Megan's swim stuff was still in the laundry room, which is odd, because she had swim that day. I thought, maybe swim is over, and she took gym clothes. But then I saw her gym bag hanging on the hook by the front door. I realized that she had forgotten what she needs for gym at school.

This is the same child that told a teacher last year that she was stabbed at a Red Lobster, and that the guy who did it was going to be getting out of jail, and she was afraid that he was going to come after her. This never happened, by the way; she just didn't want to do something that she was asked to do. This is the same child that, in sixth grade, told us (full on, with tears) in a pizza parlor that she was sent to the principal's office that day, and none of that even happened. She was just bored while we were waiting on the pizza. This is the same child that made up a boyfriend in fourth grade, because she admired a fifth-grade boy that didn't even know her, and made up stories about their interactions on the bus.

I don't think she intentionally wants to lie. I think that while I write nonfiction (because I find real life to be far crazier than fiction), she should write fiction. She has many tales stirring around up there. She spouts them off out of boredom, and when she doesn't have another creative outlet.

My theory about this phone call I received is that she also doesn't want to get into trouble with the gym teacher (who she doesn't like) because she wasn't prepared for class. Therefore, she went to talk to the guidance counselor to get out of going to gym.

This is not new. She figured out how to cut gym in kindergarten. She would just say she didn't feel good and they would send her to the nurse and she would go lay down until gym was over. Then, miraculously, she would feel fine and go back to class.

When we picked the kids up from school that day, we gave all three children a test. We made them write down the top ten things they were thankful for. Then we had them write the five things they would most like to change about their life. Then we asked them to write three things they think others think of them, and three things that they wish others thought about them.

This was all my husband's idea, by the way. I was so angry with the child, I was just going to punish her and ask questions later. It was a God thing that he was off work for the day and was home to hear me rant and rave about the situation. Thankfully, he took over, because while I wouldn't trade any of my children for all the gold in Midas, I was ready to kill her. (I wouldn't actually kill her. But as my friend Christi says, I would have liked to "send her to Jesus with a big red bow on her head." Fortunately I did have sense to marry a man that is a calming force in my life. I don't like the color orange either, so jail would be a bad idea).

Megan had to keep from smiling at some points in our little test, because she knew I was on to her. She knows I know her better than anyone, and that I won't fall for her crap. I call her on it, every time. The girls didn't take the exercise seriously, until we asked them about what they thought others thought about them, and what they wished others thought about them. We were happy that our son did take it seriously, and that he has a good head on his shoulders. Hopefully we won't run into any nonsense like this when he gets older.

It has been twenty-four hours since this little episode, and I am just now starting to get over it. As I write it out, I have to chuckle. If you don't think God has a sense of humor, you obviously haven't met our family.

Fan Girl

I'm not sure if I have ever mentioned that I'm not exactly cool or not. But...yeah, I'm not cool.

One of the cool things that has happened since my book came out (and turning that big-number birthday) is that I have been able to meet a couple of other authors and get their books signed. Granted, you can go to a book signing whether you have a book out or not, but I just never had before. In fact, it had never occurred to me that I could. Not a lot of authors have one-stoplight towns without bookstores or libraries, except for the one in the elementary school, on their book tour. I don't like to drive for longer than thirty-five minutes, either, so you see my dilemma.

Some years ago, my cousin introduced me to Jen Lancaster's books. Jen Lancaster is a Purdue grad. My husband is a Purdue grad, so automatically she is family. This woman is hilarious. She, at least in her books, is that friend you have that uses really foul language, but you love her because she makes you laugh so hard you almost pee. I want to be her best friend and drink cocktails with her after my kids are in bed. I want to float in the pool while talking about the summer reading list with her. I'm pretty sure we would be very good friends, if we were only to meet. We would meet and I would say something funny, then she would, and then we would be besties, except that isn't how it happened. Because I am an idiot.

My friend and I drove four hours to Michigan to go to her book signing and meet her. I finally am there, shaking Jen Lancaster's hand, when she thanks me for coming, and what do I say?

"No, thank YOU for coming."

Who says that? An idiot. Me. Because I. Am. An. IDIOT.

I did the same uncool "12-year-old girl meeting One Direction" thing I had done when I met Jon Acuff. Because I have not one ounce of play-it-cool mojo. I am apparently a fan girl. When we left, I needed a drink, so we stopped at a gas station to get a Coke Zero, because I was having an OK day, but not a great day. I met someone famous and I made a fool of myself kind of day. When I don't make a fool of myself, I get ice cream. (Side Note: Did you catch the Easy A reference? I have teenage daughters and little boy. All I get to watch are teenage shows and movies with superheroes. Don't judge.)

Later that night, I was recounting to my friend Kelly what I said. I groaned.

She said, "Well, when I had my turn I said, 'I like your brain.' Who says that?"

I lost it. I laughed and laughed, and laughed some more. I couldn't breathe, I was laughing so hard. Then as I was trying to fall sleep, I started to laugh again. I told her that at least maybe Jen would remember her and she might even get a tweet out of it. (So far, no such luck). So at least I wasn't the only one who went fan-girl on Jen. I feel a bit better.

I have had exactly one book signing/launch party, and I have had one speaking engagement since that time. It is not that I haven't been asked; it's only that I am not sure how to handle it. I have mentioned several times that talking in groups is way out of my comfort zone, but looking at it from someone like Jen Lancaster or Jon Acuff's point of view, I have to wonder how they handle it. They have far more experience at it, and they seem so calm and cool. I can't even *meet* someone cool without coming off like an idiot. How do they not only keep their wits about them, and handle crazy fan girls like me?

How do they go to the store without being recognized, when they just want to run in and grab some groceries and get home? I'm not sure I am ready for that kind of responsibility. I sometimes go to the store in a baseball hat and no makeup. If I were famous, you know someone would tweet that. It's the world we live in. Going undercover is hard to do.

For those who have paved the way before me, for those of you I have met, and those I have not yet had the pleasure to meet yet, I want to thank you. Thank you for being cool, even when those of us who admire you are not. You handle your responsibility with grace and that is to be admired. Sometimes (OK, usually) it is only after the fact, when I have time to think and reflect, that I start to get it. It has to be stressful, humbling, and amazing all at the same time to do what you do. I'm not there yet. Maybe I never will be.

Even if I never become a true peer (read: bestie), and I stay a fan girl, it is still cool to have the opportunity to meet someone who has accomplished much and handles it with grace. I can only hope that the more famous people I meet, the more cool may transfer over to me.

What's the Eighteenth Year?

I'm not sure how you celebrate eighteen years of marriage. Maybe you go on a cruise, or a trip to an island. Maybe you stay home and do dinner and a movie, and wait for the twenty-year anniversary. The eighteen-year anniversary gift… is it a clock, or front door, maybe? No clue.

So what did my husband and I do to celebrate this special occasion? We went to Cincinnati, Ohio. The Cincinnati Reds were not at home so we did not get to take in a game. We did, however, go to a conference to see Dave Ramsey live. Thanks to Dave's Total Money Makeover, we have changed our lives. We make much better decisions these days with our money.

So right now, you are either thinking we are big nerds, or that we are cool. Who wouldn't want to see Dave Ramsey? I have to tell you, I was stoked. But it got even better: we found out that Jon Acuff was going to be there too!

I'm not sure if you have read any of Jon's books, but you totally should. Seriously, do yourself a favor and go on Amazon and buy the entire collection. So funny, and yet really thought-provoking.

I have read all of Jon Acuff's books, and I am pretty sure that we are twins. A lot of what he says are things I say or think. When I read "Quitter," I asked my husband if he knew him, had called him and recounted my thoughts to him. When I read "Start," I realized he was a genius. While parts of it reminded me of things I think about, mostly I thought, "Wow, my little brother is so much smarter than I am."

I tell people if I had a brother, I'm pretty sure he would be Jon. Aside from the fact that he's younger, and we don't have the same parents, I am pretty sure he is the male version of me.

After the event, I had the privilege of meeting my long-lost twin, and getting a couple of his books signed. We had a conversation, and it came up that I had a book out too. So what does he ask me?

"Do you have one with you, or do you have a card?"

Of course, I had to say, "Uh…nope." I was not at all prepared for that question. It never occurred to me that anyone would ask that question, especially someone so accomplished. So my first (and maybe only) encounter with my soul brother, and when I do meet him, I'm an idiot.

The next day, we went on an adventure. We went to a grocery store. Yes, you read that right. But this was no ordinary grocery store. This place, called Jungle Jim's, is massive! It is such a huge store that they have parts of it divided up by country. In the mood for some French lemonade? Head on over to France and pick some up. How about some Mad Housewife Wine? It is in the wine section, next to the cheese. Would you like some cheese with your whine, er, wine? Maybe we only thought that was funny. I took a picture of that label, I was so amused. I'm not a big fan of wine, so my knowledge of the different brands and types is extremely limited. A wine for mad housewives. Classic!

Then we went to IKEA. I had seen an IKEA catalog, but never been to the store, or even ordered anything from the catalog. This place is amazing. You have to plan an entire day to go to that store, it is so big. Even my husband was amazed. He started talking about redecorating the house once it is paid off. Imagine, a man getting excited over home décor. They have decent prices too. You can get a meal for $1.99. We didn't get one, because we bought bakery items at the grocery store and feasted in the car before we went in. But a meal for $1.99 is practically unheard of.

People do not want to leave. The marketing people at IKEA do not want you to leave for food. They want you to stay and see everything, and picture them in your home. See the possibilities. To make it easier, everything is set up in rooms. It is genius. We bought a bookcase, and a blanket, and the softest bathmat in the tri-state area.

After all of that, we drove back closer to home, and took in a baseball game. Then we spent the night in a hotel that had no carpet, no hairdryer, and possibly the thinnest walls allowed by building inspectors. The couple right next door apparently liked to watch television. We know this because after my husband turned our television off for the night, it sounded like the sound was still on. He actually got up to inspect the television, trying to figure out why the picture was off, but the sound was still on. He even tried unplugging the television. Then we figured out it was the television from the next room, as clear as if it were our own. Then the people upstairs started walking around like elephants. So what we got was footsteps, the Home Shopping Network all night long, no hairdryer, and no mini-fridge. And no breakfast in the morning, either.

Then we spent almost an hour trying to get to a mall that was about fifteen minutes from where we had breakfast. Yes, we have a GPS, and we also had instructions from someone at the restaurant. That is how long it took us to follow directions. We got a little frustrated with each other, and then I just started cracking up. It was really quite hilarious. Only we would make it such an ordeal to get to a mall that was fifteen minutes away. But once we found it, it wasn't really all that impressive.

We attended a friend's wedding that afternoon, then we went to dinner and a movie. We went home, and were blessed by grandma with a night in our own home, alone for the night. We slept for a long time. It was fantastic.

I don't know how you celebrate eighteen years of marriage, but that is how we do it. We go see people we think highly of, we go to a grocery store, we get lost, we sleep in. It's not a Sandals vacation or anything fancy but it was so much fun.

It cements for me that this man I married is the better half. I can't wait to see the next eighteen years. I can't think of anyone else I would rather get lost with.

The 500-Month Birthday

When our children are babies, we keep track of how many months old they are, until they are about two. After two, it isn't such a big deal. The keeping track of the months goes by the wayside after that, but you know that eventually your teenage daughter is going to ask you how many months old she is.

My oldest child asked her father this spring how many months old she was. He helped her to figure it out, then, being the man that he is, he proceeded to figure out how many months old he was. It was so close to five hundred (we like round numbers) that he decided to figure out when his five hundred-month birthday would be.

As it turns out, he was going to be five hundred months old on Cinco de Mayo. Discovering this was like finding leftover pie in the fridge. We all got very excited. Then we had a reason to actually celebrate Cinco de Mayo for the very first time. He decided we should celebrate with a special dinner, and of course, he got to pick where we go. I dare you to guess where he picked. Have your ideas? Hold onto them… and now toss them out the window. We did not go to a Mexican restaurant.

We went to P.F. Changs. Why?

Because we figured they wouldn't be busy on Cinco de Mayo. Also, we have loved it ever since we discovered it last year. We have been a total of three times and were looking for an excuse to go.

I asked him to figure out when my five hundred-month birthday would be, so we could go again. This Cinco de Mayo dinner counted towards our anniversary celebration, as he turned 500 months old the day before our anniversary. Our eighteenth wedding anniversary, to be precise.

And when you put it like that, it really sounds like I'm married to an old man, or that I've robbed the cradle. "How old is your husband? He looks so young," someone might say to me.

"Oh, he is 500 months old. Why do you ask?" I could reply.

When it comes to age, I suppose perhaps we should start counting the months as we get older. After all we are getting up there, and every month seems to have a bit more significance as the months add up. How many months could we possibly be blessed with?

Although now that I give it more thought, I think when we start adding up time, it loses something. I don't want to spend my time counting them, I want to live them, no matter their number. I want to feel the blessings and acknowledge them moment by moment, not year by year, or month by month. Time wasn't meant to be counted, it was meant to be treasured.

But I'm still going to P.F. Changs.

Stretch Marks Need A New Publicist

Hello, my name is Heather, and I have stretch marks. If Victoria's Secret calls me to model for them, it will be because all of the models of the world got so hungry that they went to the Golden Corral buffet restaurant, and were never seen or heard from again.

Every time my children see commercials for stretch mark creams, they tell me that I should invest in some. I then inform my children that, if not for them, I wouldn't have the stretch marks in the first place, so we should all rejoice that I have them.

Have you seen the commercials for these creams? They are crazy. I would like to meet one mom who even has the time to think about using the cream in the first place. When I had babies, I was lucky to get five minutes to take a shower, max. Usually the baby was asleep, but you never know when they will wake up, so you go clean yourself up as quickly as possible.

It's the same way with food. To this day, I haven't slowed down when I eat. Chewing each bite thirty -two times is not an option when you are a mom, especially a new mom. If you don't even have five minutes to shower, and you spend half of your time smelling like baby spit-up, when are you going to think "Hey, I have these stretch marks to worry about. I should take care of that. Where is that cream?" Not happening. You don't have time (or the energy) for that much brain work.

Let's look at it this way. When I had my first child, I was twenty-three, and I had not one thing figured out about life. In fact, as we pulled away from the hospital with her in the backseat and me beside her, I remarked to my husband: "Wow, they really will let anyone have a baby, won't they?" We were young, and I was an only child. I knew nothing about babies. (Now I know nothing about teenagers. It's a vicious cycle. I've spent spend my entire life figuring out that I don't know anything.)

What I do have figured out is that I earned those stretch marks, darn it. I ate a lot of Ben & Jerry's to get them. I carried three children to get them. I am also not sure that anyone should be looking that closely at my body, at the age I am, to worry about what I have going on anyway. I am a married mom of three; stretch marks are the least of my problems.

Let's put some spin on this. Why not get stretch marks a new publicist? Shouldn't they be appreciated for what they represent? Can you see the headlines?

> Stretch Marks: The most meaningful tattoos you can get!

> Stretch Marks: All the cool kids are getting them!

> Stretch Marks: No ink or needles were harmed in the gaining of them!

I don't know, I'm just putting it out there. Either way, I have them, I'm not concerned. Victoria's Secret hasn't called (yet) either, so I think I'm good.

Daphne, Wallflowers, and Wanting to Die

Daphne is a huge Harry Potter fan and loves all of the actors and actresses in the movies. That said, Emma Watson was in a movie called "The Perks of Being a Wallflower." This movie did not come to our theater, so we didn't get to go see it then. When it was released on DVD, she bought it.

This movie was well made. The acting is good, and you grow to like the characters and like the friendships that are formed. But it might be one of the most depressing movies I have ever watched. I just kept looking at my daughter and saying "Really? You like this movie?"

It had Emma Watson and Logan Lerman in it. Of course, she loved it. It made me want to shoot myself or take some pills, but she loved it. There is no accounting for bad taste in movies, I guess, even if it is an all-star cast.

In thinking about the movies of my youth that I loved, I think about what drew me to them. I loved movies like "The Breakfast Club" and "Pretty in Pink" and "Sixteen Candles." When I think about what those movies were about, compared to the movies that she likes, I realize that maybe we are not so different. I loved them because the teenagers in them were outsiders, and I always felt like I was an outsider; an observer looking in at what other people's experiences were in high school. My daughter is much the same way. I was—and she is—a very quiet girl that doesn't trust a lot of people.

I suppose I haven't changed much. I may be a little louder and willing to talk to most anyone on a one-on-one basis, but I don't even ask for prayers in Sunday school class. That would require talking. I don't know why that is. I don't know if it is a lack of trust, or that I'm not sure that what I want prayer for is worthy of their time. I listen to the prayer requests from others, and I think to myself, "How can I ask people who know others who are suffering terrible diseases, or having other serious problems, or even have these issues themselves, to pray that I meet a deadline? Or that I don't get sick when I am supposed to go and speak?" I can't bring myself to do it.

I still love some of those same types of movies, the underdog movies. I like superhero movies. Movies that charge your batteries and show that anything is possible. Movies with a happy ending and leave you feeling inspired, like, "If they can do that, maybe I can too." It's about balance, and an overwhelming need to overcome adversity (even when your adversities are not as large as others').

Maybe there are actually perks to being a wallflower. But will we ever really find the magic if we are stuck in the background, like a wallflower? Flowers are meant to be centerpieces. The kids in that movie may have been wallflowers by movie standards, but they had a group of friends that pulled them off the wall and brought them to the center of the dance floor. Even the wallflowers eventually find their way to be centerpieces.

I guess the movies Daphne picks out aren't so off the wall after all. She also likes all the movies with the singing and dancing, and belts out the tunes right along with them.

It's OK that we watch movies that have a message we are looking for. But shouldn't we already know that we can find the same message from our Father in Heaven? God cares about all of our troubles. There isn't anything we cannot bring to Him and find that He will lead us to where He wants us. All of his plans are perfect. Even for us mistrusting wallflower types.

It's Elementary, My Dear

I graduated from preschool at the end of the last school year. This year I moved up to kindergarten. While I enjoyed my time at the preschool, working with great people and some great kids, I am happy to report that I love kindergarten even more.

The building I work in is close to home, and that is handy for a girl who hates to drive, especially in the winter. The people that I work with are amazing. It is an honor to be surrounded by such caring people, who also enjoy a good joke.

I enjoy dressing up to go to work. I am an accessorizing kind of gal, so in the winter I wear a lot of scarves. One of the gals at work has taken notice of this and decided that there should be another name for my scarves.

"What's another name for a scarf?" she asked.

I said, "I don't know... a noose?"

She started laughing and decided that the "Nestleroad noose" was a great name for it. So for work I wear slacks, a sweater, dress shoes, and my "Nestleroad noose." Perhaps that could be my trademark. For some people it is their hair, or a certain shirt, but for me, it could be my scarf. But how to choose just one would be the problem.
I have several.

Confession: I have a love affair going with the laminator.
In preschool, I didn't get to laminate anything. In kindergarten, I

get to laminate a lot. The laminator is in a workroom that is a bit secluded. It is quiet and warm in there with the laminator on, and ninety-eight percent of the time that I am in there, I am alone. Not that I mind working with other people. But it is a bit of a respite, if you will, and it soothes me to feed the papers into the machine. A bit of therapy in the middle of a crowded day.

My next love with an inanimate technological device would have to be with the copier. The first time I used it, it was love. This new copier is massive, and it is amazing! This machine can sort and group, and it tells you the difference between the two. It also offsets and staples and hole punches. I love this copier. It is my left hand at work. I cannot do my job without this copier. I get so excited to use the copier that I volunteer to make copies for other people. It beats doing dishes and sweeping floors any day of the week.

I get to walk backwards when taking the kids to all of their different locations. I tell them that they have to have a whistle to be able to walk backwards. That is another thing that I get excited about with this job. I was given not only a key to get in the door in the morning, but also a whistle. I waited forty years to be given a whistle. When I received my whistle, it was like Christmas morning. Walking backwards (so I can keep an eye on all of the kids) is a perk that comes with the whistle.

When I was in kindergarten, I wanted to be a kindergarten teacher. My dreams changed as I got older. I am still not the kindergarten teacher, but I think I would rather be doing what I am doing. I have the best of both worlds. I get to work with the kids, but I still get time spend time with my own children.

God's planning is always perfect. I am always amazed at the blessings that He has given to me and is still giving me. I don't know what next year has in store for me but I don't dwell on it, either. Until then, I am enjoying every minute of kindergarten. I have never been so excited to go to work.

Counting Chickens

When I worked at the preschool, in the springtime we would put eggs in an incubator. The children would watch every day in anticipation for the eggs to hatch.

I'm not a farm girl. The only farms I have ever been to were on field trips. And my eggs come from the grocery store. The process of the incubator and the eggs hatching, however, intrigued me. I was fascinated. The thing about chickens is that when they hatch and fluff out to little chicks, they are so cute. This cuteness lasts about a week. By the end of the second week, they are no longer cute, and they smell… bad.

I am a self-professed foodie. I love food. I don't, however, want to know where it comes from. I don't want to make friends with the animals that my food comes from. It just seems wrong. I get that killing animals is necessary for food. I don't want to be the one who does it, nor do I want to know anything about how it is done. I will just continue to think that chicken comes from the freezer department of the grocery store. I'm good with that.

The children would count the eggs and the chicks when they hatched. It was a good math exercise for the kids, but "food for thought" for me. Counting chickens before they hatch. How many times have you heard that expression? I have heard it as recently as last week. We don't want to count our chickens before they hatch. We don't want to get our hopes up. We don't want to be disappointed if it doesn't work out. What would happen if we went ahead and counted them anyway?

Take Noah, for example. Noah counted his chickens and just believed. He believed so much, that he built an ark for rain that was coming. Rain like no one had ever seen. So naturally, everyone thought he was nuts. He didn't worry about if all the chickens would hatch. In fact, he didn't just count chickens. He counted two of every kind of animal on Earth. Loaded all of them up on the ark he built and held tight for the greatest storm the earth had ever seen. God said he would flood the Earth, and Noah said ok. He didn't question; he just went with it.

Ruth went with Naomi to Naomi's homeland, far from where her people were. Naomi told Ruth and Orpah to turn back and go back to their people. Orpah went back and rejoined her people, but Ruth clung to Naomi and refused to leave her. She didn't think over all of her options. She didn't hesitate. She clung to Naomi and went with her. I don't think she thought "Hmm, well... you have a point. Maybe I should go back and find me a man and worship my false gods, just in case Naomi is crazy." No. She said, "Where you go, I will go." She counted on every one of those chickens to hatch.

What would happen if we just believed? What if God said "jump," and we just started jumping, instead of asking "OK, God, how high and how fast and for how long?" What if we just started jumping, and then listened to God for further instructions? Can you imagine? What if we counted every one of those chickens before they hatched? What if we completely relied on God to provide? Has God not promised that he has "plans to give you hope and a future"? (Jeremiah 29:11) I think that means we can count every one of those little chickens, and God will provide. He will not forsake us. He loves us.

So I'm over here counting chickens. Kind of like counting sheep, only you know, without actual chickens or sheep. Counting some blessings instead, and realizing that each of them is a gift from God. Our God is awesome; there is nothing that is too big for Him to handle. He created the heavens and the Earth. I'm counting — are you?

Thankful

I get that people want to express their gratitude, the week or month of Thanksgiving, on all the social networks for the world to see. But I have never been able to figure out how one chooses just one thing to be thankful for each day. But I find myself wondering about the rest of the year.

It is great to be thankful in November. But keep being thankful clear 'til New Years is over (when you haven't kept up with the resolutions, and you find that cake still tastes good in February. Of course, I say be thankful for cake, too). My intent here is not to downplay any of it, but what about the rest of the year? Are you thankful then, too? Are you conscious of the fact that on June fifth, what a blessing it is to wake up that day?

I went through a bit of a spiritual overhaul at some point. I made a conscious decision to be thankful and find the blessings in everyday life. Good day or bad, whether I was running late or had a stomach issue, no matter if there was sunshine or rain, I will recognize that I wasn't promised to live that day. That no matter what, I will be thankful.

I would hope that in talking to me, especially when you're asking me about my family and friends, you would see my eyes light up when I speak about them. I would hope that when you ask me about the journey God has set me on. You would notice the sheer awe I have about God's decision to use me. I am well aware of the fact that I am no one special and that there are others more qualified to do what I do, and yet here I sit with tears flowing, because He chose me. Me? I am ill-equipped, I stumble over my words, I am weepy, and I fail to be somebody anyone would choose for work of great importance.

I have often wondered what others see when they meet me. What I want others to see when they meet me is my thankfulness and love for God's blessings in my life. I want for nothing. I am blessed beyond measure. To choose just one thing per day to be thankful for would be impossible for me. I could no sooner choose a star from the sky or a book from my shelf.

I don't know if I can even choose something to not be thankful for, although it may be easier. But even then, what would I choose? My gray hair? I don't think so; I earned every one of those silver sparklers! I do have hair color, so who am I to complain?

Should I choose my stretch marks, which my loving children recommended I buy cream to get rid of? I earned each of those too, carrying three of the best blessings God ever granted me.

How about the extra pounds? Even those I enjoyed gaining. Sure, I could do without them, and I am getting close to being annoyed enough to start shedding them ... but whose fault were they? The bakers of the world, or the Mexican food restaurant I enjoy so much? Food is not necessarily something to be unthankful for; it's more something to take control of.

Arguing with the kids? Nope. I argued with my mother until some of her last days, and I miss it. Arguing is better than indifference any day. Disagreements can spark learning and understanding. Even for those, I am thankful.

So to answer those who may wonder why, even though I write, yet I don't participate in a "thankful a day" social media plan: yes, I am thankful. Abundantly so. The amount of thankfulness in my heart is overflowing. When you give each day to God and ask him to bless it, how could your heart not be thankful?

Laser Tag

Over spring break, we were unable to do any traveling, because my husband had to work, and we didn't have enough cash saved up to go anywhere, anyway. So we decided to go to play laser tag with the kids.

We had had a good week together, but for a couple of days we were snowed in due to a crazy spring snowstorm (with more than 10 inches of snow). Being cooped up had worn on everyone, so we were hoping to be able to take out our aggression on each other. Ideally, we would have been the only ones there and we would not have been on teams, but fighting against each other. This did not happen.

First, a bit of advice: Do not tell people you are going to go shoot people with lasers unless you are sure everyone on your Facebook page knows you well, and they know that shooting people with lasers is legal, and a good stress reliever. If you do announce this bit of fun information, and you have an uncle like mine, you will be told basically that you are bad person. Do not take this too much to heart.

When we got there, we found out that there would be another fifteen to twenty people in this game, and that as a family, we would all be on the same team. We were given instructions on how to put the equipment on, and what to do and what not to do. Apparently running from people trying to tag you is a no-no. This goes against the fight or flight instinct, I say.

I wasn't too concerned, though, because my dad was a Marine. In my attempt to psych out the kids that I was going to win this event, I had told them that I would win because I surely had some innate instinct in this area. I have never held a gun before (laser or otherwise), but this didn't concern me. I come from a line of military people. I just assumed that it would be in my blood. That, and the fact that I have dreams of being a ninja and saving the world, had me convinced that laser tag would not be a problem.

As it turns out, the girls, who I had wanted to tag, stuck to me like glue. I had to keep telling them to hold the sensor when they went to shoot or it wouldn't work. Every idea I had about being good at this game went downhill, as the majority of the game I spent tagged and recharging. There wasn't a site on the gun. You couldn't tell where you were shooting. That was only part of the problem.

I noticed an older grey-haired gentleman, who apparently spends a great deal of time there with his family, as this was their second game of the day. Maybe he once was a Marine, too, as he popped up everywhere and mowed us all down. Between him and the little kids who came up to my waist and snuck up on me and tagged me before I knew what was happening, I didn't stand a chance.

Vaughn took off and I didn't see him the entire time we were in there. Scotty took off and I came across him just once. He was with a girl from another family that was on our team. They took off to take out a tower or something, and I never saw him again until the game was over. To tell you the truth, I'm not completely certain that the boys of our group weren't the ones hiding and taking us girls out half the time. But when we went to pick up our score cards, we found out that we were the five worst players in the game. Daphne was the worst of everyone, and I was right behind her.

We had a good time playing laser tag, though, and with the coupon they had on their website, it cost us less than going to a movie. Of course, that may be because we only played the one game. When we left, the older guy that had been shooting all of us was back in line, waiting for another round with his family.

Having family in the military does not actually help in your ability to play laser tag. Neither does reading books, or seeing the movies based on books.

I have a friend whose husband knows how to shoot bow and arrows. At one point this summer, they said they would take me out in the yard and let me give it a try. I was pretty sure I was going to be good at it. I have seen "The Hunger Games" several times. In "The Princess Diaries 2," they shoot bow and arrows too. I studied the technique. Even though I have never actually seen a bow and arrow in person, I did see the mother of all bow and arrows on "Pawn Stars" once.

But just in case the back yard may not be a good idea, we may need to go into a field and make sure no livestock is in the way. Steel-toed shoes may be a good idea also.

This should be fun, don't you think?

Toothbrushes

There were sixteen toothbrushes residing in my house. There are five people and two cats that live here. The cats don't do anything in the bathroom but drink out of the toilet (weird, I know, I thought that was a dog thing). The point is that they don't brush their teeth, what with the lack of thumbs and all.

So between the five humans living in this house, we have sixteen toothbrushes. I will claim two of them. I am not sure what the other four people have going on. We all received (in our Christmas stockings; I thought they went well with the candy) new battery-operated spin toothbrushes. So shouldn't all other toothbrushes have become obsolete?

This last weekend I planned a family meeting (or, a come to Jesus meeting) to discuss this very issue. I have to ask why we are holding on to so many toothbrushes. We make regular dental visits. Every time, we get a new toothbrush.

Are they scared of throwing away the old one? Afraid of hurting its feelings, maybe? Afraid they won't like the new one as well? The old one is broken in and the new one may not clean to their liking? Whatever the reason, some of these toothbrushes are going to have to go. The last time I checked, there wasn't a toothbrush shortage, so there's no reason to hoard them.

On Sunday afternoon, we called a meeting in the kitchen. We then all went to each of the bathrooms and ceremoniously threw away extra toothbrushes. I think we cut the number in half. Three of us insisted that they had to have a regular toothbrush as well as a spinning toothbrush.

Now I wonder what else we have accumulated that we need to cut down on. I suppose I shouldn't have to look far. Last night when tucking my son into bed, he informed me that he needed another bookshelf. His books are all over his room and need a home.
I said perhaps we need to just box up some of the books from the bookshelf, and make room for the ones that are actually in use. We still have Junie B. Jones books on our shelves. No one is reading them. I don't want to throw them away, but I think that perhaps they can go in the attic for when I have grandchildren to read them to. Those are classic books. Why re-buy books?

What are you holding onto that you can let go? It occurs to me that, just like extra toothbrushes and books, sometimes we accumulate hurts and wrongs and failures that we need to just let go of. Why do we insist on holding onto things that only cause us harm, and do not bring us closer to our God? Who are we not forgiving? We only hurt ourselves when we fail to forgive. What good does that do?

Like my daughter does, when I was younger, I held onto everything that hurt me. As a teenage girl, you hold things, and tend to believe lies before truth. She remembers things from so long ago, no one else can possibly remember the things she is still upset about. I tend to float in oblivion. If someone doesn't like me, I either don't know about it or I fail to care. I realize at this point that not everyone is going to like me. I'm kind of an acquired taste. That's OK, because God loves me and He has big plans for me. I live my life to please him and not the people who would choose to judge me. Also, I tend to assume at this point that people will like me. God likes me, and if I have done nothing to harm someone, what point would it be to not like me?

I learned all of this far past my high school years. Try as I might to teach these lessons to my girls, I fail. If someone is mean to them, they are broken. I am learning that they too, will have to learn these things on their own. And they too are going to have to learn to lean on the ONE that can guide them through any situation.

I think the point of any excess is to at least be aware of it, then accept the trimming and the cutting. Whether that's a new clean bathroom, or a new creation in Christ.

Time Keeps on Slipping, Slipping

This morning I found myself crying while getting ready for work. It occurred to me that it was Friday. While I am excited about it being the end of the week, I am also very distraught about it being the end of another week. The time seems to pass so quickly now. Time is a funny thing, isn't it? When we are younger we can't wait to grow up, and move on with our lives, and as we get older we only wish for more time.

My daughter is a senior. Yesterday she brought home order forms for graduation invites, thank you cards, and all the other things that apparently we must have in order to graduate. It was then that I realized, this is really happening. Yesterday, she was just a cute little blonde in pigtails telling me she was a big girl and that she had to get on the bus to go to school. I remember it so clearly; then I blinked, and now this young lady is preparing to move on to the next phase of her life.

I asked her this morning if it was OK for me to be excited for her, and yet sad for me. She will be leaving to go to college and her sister won't be far behind her. Their brother, who was our surprise child, will be the only one left for me run around and do mother things for. We will have a lot fewer school functions and homework. I have no idea how to prepare a meal for only three people.

I think I am afraid of the time slipping away mostly because I haven't yet figured out what my life is going to look like once they are all gone. What if we're alone and have no one else to take care of, and my husband decides he doesn't like me? When we have no one to team up against, in a battle between us and the kids; what then?

My husband is very self-reliant, and is so much smarter than I am. He doesn't need me to do anything for him. He can survive without me. The realization that my children are no longer going to need me either is terrifying. If I'm not needed, what is my purpose in life? What do I do with my time? The fact of the matter is that perhaps they have never needed me as much as I have needed them. Is that sad? It might be.

As we all approach these next milestones, I have had some self-discovery. Interesting how we continually search for ourselves long after we are adults, and yet what do we really need to know? How much do we need to know about ourselves that we cannot find out from God?

As I think about all of the changes and the unknown, I hear a whisper of a song from my internal playlist. Matthew West and his song "Hello My Name is Child of the One True King" plays in my head. Maybe that is the journey, the journey for all of us is to discover who we are in Christ. Not to dwell on the unknown, but put our trust in Him who understands.

The History Channel

I am a sitcom girl. I grew up on them. I loved family shows, the funny ones that still had a good solid message. Right up my alley. To this day, I love the old shows, and a few that are on today. I also enjoy a drama or two, but I have never been a history buff. Until recently.

I blame Tom Hanks. He created "Band of Brothers," which I loved. Then we watched "The Pacific," which I didn't love, but I liked. And then we discovered "Pawn Stars." Well, my husband discovered it and introduced it to me. Now I find myself watching that, "Counting Cars," and "American Restoration."

I have no idea what has happened to me. When did I become a woman who enjoyed watching war mini-series, and what I would classify as boy shows? I don't know a thing about cars; I rarely even enjoy driving. I've never even been to a pawn shop. The oldest thing I own is a picture of my great-grandmother. I do have my eye on a pair of vintage-looking shoes, but that is a girly thing to be interested in. (Black and white spectator shoes. Love!)

As I was watching a Counting Cars marathon, I was trying to put my finger on just what the draw was. Then I realized: they are making old things new again. How do you not like a show like that?

Who would have thought watching one of these shows would have brought forth any sort of insight at all? But this is what Jesus does for us—he makes old things new. He makes us new.

They bring cars in to the shop, rusted out, without engines, they make them look and work like new. They bring antiques into a pawn shop that seem worthless, but find out that they are rare and valuable items. They take all sorts of things to the restoration shop and they… restore them.

Jesus took the broken, the downtrodden, the tax collectors, the pagans, the prostitutes, the sick, even the dead, and he makes them new. He didn't come for the perfect people; he was the only one who was perfect. He wasn't even seeking the almost-perfect; he was looking to make things new. He came to save the weak, to show grace and mercy to his children, and to save us from our own destruction. We are a broken people, but Jesus can make us new. There is no better message.

That is our history. The Bible is our history. The good news is that we don't have to be history, but our brokenness can be. We can be made new with our faith in Jesus.

Old things made new. Love.

What Kind of Christian?

I am a believer in Christ. I believe that Jesus died on a cross, and took the punishment for my sins. My sins are many. If ever anyone needed a savior, it was and still is me. I am forgiven. What does that mean? I can tell you, it doesn't mean that I am perfect. It doesn't mean that I now get to play judge and jury. There is only one judge.

As Christians, that is sometimes where we run into trouble. We start comparing our sins.

"Well, look at her, she is an alcoholic. At least I'm not that."

"Look at him—he is a murderer! At least I never killed anyone."

"Look at her, she had an affair! At least I never did that."

"Look at him, he curses like a truck driver [I don't know any truck drivers, so I don't actually know how they talk. I only know the expression.] He even takes the Lord's name in vain!"

"Look at them, they are living in sin."

"Look at them—they only go to church on holidays."

Seriously? It's disgusting and embarrassing. Or when we get into "They got what they deserved." That's a big one, too. As if we should - or even could - decide their punishment. No wonder non-believers don't want to be told the gospel. They aren't hearing the truth of Jesus from our mouths when we talk like this.

The message of Jesus is not one of condemnation. If God wanted to condemn the entire world instead of save it, he wouldn't have sent his son. He would have just burned it up, or sent another flood to destroy it, and started over again. Have we not learned yet?

The message of Jesus is that of grace and mercy. There is example after example of God's grace and mercy.

(Micah 7:18): "Who is a God like you, who pardons sin and forgives the transgression of the remnant of his inheritance? You do not stay angry forever but delight to show mercy."

We are expected to show grace, too. (Luke 6:36): "Be merciful, just as your Father is merciful."

So what are we doing? Are we forgetting that God sees a sin as a sin? Even the thought of another that is not your spouse is considered adultery? Being angry or holding a grudge is a sin?

Romans 3:23-24 says: "For all have sinned and fall short of the glory of God, and are justified freely by his grace through the redemption that came by Christ Jesus."

Did you get that? ALL of us have fallen short of the glory of God. That is me, that is you, that is everyone you have ever met, and even the ones you haven't. The good news is that we are justified by his grace and the redemption that came by Jesus. Grace. The message of Jesus is grace and mercy.

I am so thankful that I don't have to worry about judgment from those who compare my sins to theirs, simply to make themselves feel better. I choose Jesus. I choose a message of grace and mercy and love from the One who makes all things new and beautiful, even knowing full well how broken I am. That is the kind of Christian I want to be. The kind of Christian that shows grace and mercy and love to others, and shows others the grace that I have been shown, just by spreading the love of my Lord and Savior.

He is worthy. We are not. We shouldn't lose sight of that.

What kind of Christian will you be?

Wardrobe Malfunction

This week at work I had a wardrobe malfunction. My first thought was, I wonder how Janet Jackson would handle this situation. I mention her only because of the area in which I was having the malfunction.

While I didn't actually reveal any skin, I did happen to notice that I was a little more, let's say, comfortable than I should have been. I looked down and noticed that one side was hanging a bit lower than the other side. (At which point, the song "Do your ears hang low, do they wobble to and fro?" played in my head.) The problem was that I had no time to go and try to figure out the problem. I chose to ignore it and to stay busy. That way no one would notice that anything was out of sorts.

After going to lunch with a friend, and then to the store (I kept my coat on), I got home where I could properly investigate. The bra that I had chosen in the dark that morning was having issues. One wire in, one wire out, then somewhere in the course of the day, the strap broke too. Not came undone -- as it was a convertible bra that could be switched around --- no, it just plain broke. This was the straw that broke the bra's strap, and it was retired to the trash. I will be shopping for a new favorite very soon.

I asked the teacher I work with the next day if she had noticed my wardrobe malfunction. She hadn't. Which leaves me with the question: Which is worse: having a wardrobe malfunction of this magnitude, or having one, but no one can tell? Think about it.

I injured myself twice in the past two weeks, both times while attempting to prepare dinner. The first time, I couldn't find the can opener that should have been in the countertop kitchen tool spinny thing (the technical name for it). I proceeded to go searching through drawers to find it, and sliced open my thumb on an apple corer (it's sharp without its cover, which is probably also hiding in the drawer). Then I whacked the top of my hand on the corner of the counter, so I got to go to school with a round bandage on my hand; you know, the kind you would put over a wart (Hello granny, can I help you?).

So as you can see, I'm very gifted when it comes to food preparation and all things domestic. Not. Shall we discuss how I keep putting clothes in the dryer, in an attempt to remove wrinkles from our clothes, because if I use the iron, I will burn myself? I am incapable of ironing without causing bodily harm. This would also be why I have short hair, so I don't have to go near a curling iron.

I find all of it quite amusing. I am accident-prone obviously, but I am also very blessed. Even with all the silliness that is my life, it all makes sense to me because I know I'm in the right spot with all the right people.

Joyful

If I could choose a word to be my word, that is the one I would choose. Joyful just inspires happiness.

I figured something out a while ago. I get to choose my attitude. I can choose to be grumpy or sad or mean, or I can choose joy. I also figured out that I am not here to work for myself. The moment I chose that I was going to give each and every day to God, I found that I am so much happier. I am joyful. My heart feels lighter.

That is not to say that I don't get frustrated, or that I don't get my feelings hurt; I absolutely do. I am the mother of two teenage daughters. But even with all the heartbreak that comes with raising teenage girls—because, let's face it, at least one week out of the month there are things that come out of their mouths that cannot be from God—I am reminded that this too shall pass. Even when part of me wants to just run away, I find my feet are planted. I can't run even if I wanted to. It seems I am rooted to this place to teach and to guide them so they can find their joy in Jesus.

Still, there are many things in this world that I fail to understand. Like sports. I don't get it. I'm not a sporty girl, I don't see why people take them so seriously. They're just games. If people put that much passion in their families and in God, families would stay together, and joy would be the predominant mood in our culture, instead of competition.

Guns. I don't get that either. How can something that was created to cause harm to others bring one joy? But then I also do not understand the differences between all the different types of onions. So I think maybe I'm not meant to understand everything. If you haven't figured it out yet, I question everything, knowing that even if I am given the answer, I still may not understand it. That's OK.

Each day at school we are given a moment of silence where we are able to pray if we so choose to. I choose to pray. I take whatever opportunity I can. My prayer daily is that my every thought, word, and action will be a reflection of God's love, and that I may be a light to bring others to get to know Him. I pray that my kids have good days at school and that my husband and I are able to do well at our jobs. (We don't get long, so I have to pray fast.) Each day I go to work, I am joyful. I enjoy being there. I feel the blessing that it is to have a job that brings me joy.

It does not escape my notice that I am blessed in many ways. Even when I look back at all of the pain and heartache that I have endured in this life, God has used all of it to bring me here, to this place, where joy is the predominate mood in my heart, mind and soul.

Lost & Found, or, a Word from the Author

You cannot see people for who they are, or who they are becoming, if you are too busy focusing on who they once were.

That is the thought that occurs to me as I realize no one in my family (outside of the people in my house) understands what it is that I do. I'm not sure if even most of my friends understand it. I'm just getting a grasp on it myself.

I started writing some time ago, almost by accident. A neighbor suggested that I start a blog. Blogs were the thing to do, apparently; I didn't have a clue about them until then. But somehow, Nestled In Suburbia was born. I looked at some other blogs to get an idea of what it is you were supposed to do with a blog. I then started telling stories about the kids and our family.

I didn't blog all the time; just every now and then. As time went on, I started blogging more. The stories became longer, and turned to different things I was learning. Then one day, three years later, I was standing in a kitchen talking to a friend about writing, and that was the beginning of my first book.

I don't know how I got here. I don't know how this happened. I was just seeing what this blog thing was about; I wasn't even very experienced with Facebook at the time. Half the time when I write, I don't know what I'm going to write about.

Then there are times when I go back and read things that I have written, and I'm surprised that I was the one who wrote it. Sometimes even though it is my fingers on the keys, maybe I am not the one writing. Maybe I am just writing what God is giving me, because he has something he wants me to convey. He has decided to use me (a very big mess of a person) to deliver some message he thinks will be best heard from someone like me. And now I am not only on Facebook, but I have my personal page AND my author page.

I don't know what I am really supposed to be doing. All I do know is that I was looking for something. I was walking through life, but I wasn't seeing everything, and when I began writing, I started noticing more. I started paying more attention. After I had my blog, having lunch with a group of friends at a restaurant that serves beautiful food isn't just lunch with a group of friends. It is a story, a story of people coming together and sharing common interests, even if it is a love of food and a silly British accent.

In looking and noticing what was around me, I started getting to know myself. I also started getting to know my God better, and how he loves me. It is then that I re-read things that my fingers typed out, but the words don't seem like me. That's when I know that it is God working through me to accomplish something that I don't fully understand.

All of life is a get-to-know-you session. Getting to know God, getting to know who we are, and getting to know and see who we could be if we let go and let Him take over. If we let him work some miracles in our lives.

I think that miracles happen every day. We just get so busy that we don't notice them all. Maybe we expect all miracles to be huge, gigantic gestures or happenings. Sometimes a miracle is just a family staying together. A couple of teenage girls getting along without fighting for an entire twenty-four hour period; a meal you have never prepared before turning out right; finding a swimsuit or a dress that actually fits you. Miracles definitely don't have to be huge. The miracle is in noticing the small blessings, so you can see (and appreciate) the big ones when they come.

I was lost there for a while. I was floundering around, trying to find my way. I fell in a pit for a couple of years, only to fall in another one three years later. I fell into the trap of focusing on all of the things that I had lost, instead of focusing on the miracles that I still had.

I am a mother to three healthy, wondrous children. I love these children more than I even knew I was capable of. I even love the little kids at school. They are miracles — each and every one of them. I love seeing their little minds work. I love seeing them make connections, and seeing the light in their eyes when they grasp a new concept. It's miraculous. I am awed that I get to be there to witness how God grows them each day.

Writing helped me find myself in the rubble. Somewhere along the way, God took over and decided he had a plan for me. I still don't know all of the plan. I only know that I am not who I once was. You may look at me and see me as the smart-mouth kid that drove my mother nuts. You may look at me and see the mother who can turn on a dime in the middle of a busy restaurant and put her kids in their place. You may see me as the woman who once had to carry a screaming toddler out of the mall and leave without a holiday dress because said toddler wanted to get naked in the middle of the store. You may see me as the woman that fell in the pit and ran from God and tried to hide away at a couple of points. You may see me as the last one in the neighborhood to mow the yard. I don't know how you see me.

If I think about it, I guess I don't really care. Somewhere along the way, typing on the keys, I found myself again. It was then that I felt my God had never left me, and I ran back into his arms. I realized it only matters how He sees me. I don't seek anyone's approval but His.

If you are so focused on who I once was, you may just miss out on my miracle: the miracle that is ME. Because I am a miracle, God saved me. He has a plan for me, and to have that happen still, that to me is a miracle.

I am not who I once was, because I am a work in progress. The progress is slow, but I find that I am relinquishing more and more control. I am being asked to do more things that I said I would never want to do, but God says go do it. So I am going.

Acknowledgements

First and foremost, I want to thank my Lord and Savior Jesus. Without God, I am an aimless wanderer in a very scary world. I hope I am fulfilling your purpose for my life. To you goes all glory!

I have the best husband and partner in life in Vaughn. Thank you for your endless support and putting up with me for all of these years. It isn't easy, I know. You are my better half. God blessed me with you.

My children are my muse. Daphne, you are such an adventure. Your help and inspirations make this possible. I love you to the moon and back. Megan, your creativity and background music fill my heart. Scotty, you have such a quick wit and contagious laugh and fun personality. Our family was made complete when you came into it. I am nothing without the three of you. You are proof that God's plans are better than our own.

My best friend Christi is the strongest person I know. I know this because I am exasperating (I looked it up) and she continues to be the best cheerleader and the woman I admire most as a friend and woman of Christ.

None of this is possible without Shannon Janeczek, who is the best editor and publisher. I am also blessed to call her my friend. Your belief in me is one reason this was possible. Thank you for being you.

I have such cool book covers, and that is because of a talented graphic designer. Karen Nowosatko, you did it again! You are going to be more famous than David Hasselhoff in Germany.

I am so excited about having pictures in this book. I have no artistic ability whatsoever. These awesome pictures are because I have a talented artist friend in Elizabeth Harner. You are a blessing to our family and your German chocolate cake has ruined all cake for me forever. Martha has nothing on your many abilities.

I may not have my love of the written word without my grandmother, Mary Lou Myers. For that I am eternally grateful. I love you, grandma.

My crazy cats are a part of our family. I'm told that I should thank them too, as they felt slighted the first time around. You shed everywhere and I think you might be forcing us to feed all of the neighborhood cats too, but we love you. You make great guard cats and napping buddies.

And last but not least, my readers. I hope you enjoy this as much as I do and God has used me to get His message across to all of you.

God bless you!

About the Author

Heather Nestleroad was born in a small Midwestern town to parents who loved each other, until they didn't anymore.

She then spent the rest of her childhood watching family shows and dreaming of one day having a family just like on TV. After getting married and having children, one day she discovered she did have a family like that, only funnier. Heather now lives in yet another small Midwestern town with her husband, three children, and two cats.

When she isn't writing about the hilarity in her own life, she is working with kindergartners, going to Bible study, driving her children to various destinations, searching for the best place to have lunch, and looking for ways to get out of cooking dinner.

You can visit her at her blog: NestledinSuburbia.com.

www.ingramcontent.com/pod-product-compliance
Lightning Source LLC
LaVergne TN
LVHW051728080426
835511LV00018B/2945